DAN███████████████████████████ Gabon, in 1967.
He h█████████████████████████ in Gabon, an MA
from ████████████████████████ nD and another MA
from t████████████████ is currently an
Associat██ ████ ██ ██ ench and █ cophone Studies in the
Departm███ ██ █ ench, German and Russian at Montclair State
University, Montclair, USA. He is the Executive Director of
SORAC (Society of Research on African Cultures) and the
Editor-in-Chief of the *SORAC Journal of African Studies*. He
has published several articles in the areas of francophone, post-
colonial and African studies. He is the author of *La
représentation des groupes sociaux chez les romanciers noirs
sud-africains* (L'Harmattan, 1996), and *Images of Africa:
Stereotypes and Realities* (Africa World Press, 2001). He also
leads the BDP (Bongo Doit Partir), a political organization
which sets itself in opposition to the Omar Bongo regime and
which promotes democracy and democratic reforms in Gabon.

DANIEL MENGARA

MEMA

Heinemann

Heinemann Educational Publishers
Halley Court, Jordan Hill, Oxford OX2 8EJ
A part of Harcourt Education Limited

OXFORD   MELBOURNE   AUCKLAND
JOHANNESBURG   GABORONE   KUALA LUMPUR
PORTSMOUTH (NH) USA   CHICAGO

ISBN 0 435 90923 1

07 06 05 04 03
10 9 8 7 6 5 4 3 2 1

British Library Cataloguing in Publication Data
A full catalogue record for this book is available from the British Library.

CIP data is on file with the Library of Congress.

Phototypeset by SetSystems Ltd, Saffron Walden, Essex
Printed and bound in Great Britain by
Cox and Wyman Ltd, Reading, Berkshire

I remember.

I remember Mema.

Mother. My mother.

My mother was a strong woman. I remember her. I remember everything. I remember her words, her story, her life, her pains, her tribulations and joys. I remember everything as if it happened yesterday. How old was she? I cannot tell with certainty because, like all people of her generation who were born before the freeing of our country from the rule of the Fulassi people, she was born 'around . . .' That is, around an obscure year that no one seems to be able to remember. Her age is therefore a guess, for no one knows exactly. But does it matter, really? No. Not to me. All that matters is that she was my mother. Why do I keep saying 'was'? Should I not say 'is'? In my village, the elders say that one can never say that the person standing over there was my father. Because blood relationships never end and can never be broken, we were all told as children that we could only use 'is' when talking about blood ties. So, I should probably be using 'is' when telling strangers about my mother. But you understand. This language I use to remember and tell the story of my mother is hard to master. It forces me to say 'was'. This language is as forceful as the language of the Fulassi people.

The Fulassi are white people, just like the Dzaman and the Nguess. They are all merciless conquerors who took over our lands. My mother used to tell me about the authority of the Fulassi, who were very severe with us black people and forced

1

everyone to learn their language and obey their laws. When one did not obey their laws, one was often beaten to death. Some youths were taken from villages for no reason and sent to work for the white man, who was building roads. He needed to build roads because he was cutting down big trees that he wanted to send back home for his people to use in the land of the Fulassi. My mother told me no one was paid for this, and several people from my village who were taken away never came back. Old people thought they did not return because they had died. My mother often heard stories of people being chained together as prisoners because the white man did not want anyone leaving work.

White people are really strange people, my mother used to tell me. She thought they were crazy. When you parted from them at night, you could never tell what they were going to do the next day. They could wake up one day and decide that it was time for them to go to war. This is how, one day, the chief of the white tribe we called Dzaman suddenly woke up, and decided that he needed to take over the lands of all the other white tribes who did not speak his language. This is how the Fulassi who ruled our land and the Dzaman started to fight a big war against each other. The war became even bigger when all the other white tribes took sides. So, my mother recalled, when the war broke out between the Fulassi and the Dzaman, one of the Fulassi chiefs did not want to let the Dzaman rule his land. This chief, whom my mother remembers as 'Gol', was desperate. The Dzaman had taken his land very quickly, so he sought refuge in the land of the Nguess who helped him with the war. Because Gol, the Fulassi chief, had now become aware of the pain one feels when one's land is taken over by strangers, he promised us to leave us alone in our lands if we helped his people win the war against the Dzaman. Some of our people went to the land of the Fulassi to help them free their people.

Most of our people who went there never came back. My mother heard strange stories of how some of our brothers died in the white man's war. Others, she remembered, were said to have become crazy after the war and ended up roaming the streets of the white man's towns like ghosts. Some were brought back to us, but they were no longer the same.

So, after the war, this Fulassi chief named Gol took his country back from the Dzaman people. He was so happy with the help of our people that he kept his promise and gave our lands back to us. The land where my people lived took on a new name. My mother told me this name was 'Ngabon', and we all became 'Ngabonê'. Other parts of the big land that the white people called 'Aferika' took their own names too. Black people were very happy. They called this moment of freedom 'independence'. The people who speak my language in Ngabon even created a dance called 'Gol' in memory of the white Fulassi chief who kept his promise and gave us our land back.

The people in my village used to say that a people without land was like a child without a mother. A child was able to know who he was, where he came from and where he was going only when he had a mother. Without a mother, the villagers said, a child was lost. He was lost because he knew neither his past, nor his present. In order for a child to know who he was, he needed to know his past. The past told him why his present was as it was. The past was the key to his present. He could unlock the truths of the present only when he used his past as the key to those truths. The same was true with regard to the future. For, if one does not have a past, then one cannot have a present. And if one has no present, then the doors to the future are locked.

So, I am lucky that I still have my mother. I am lucky that I have her in my head. I am happy that I can still hear her words in my ears, even when I am far away. Mema cannot die. She will never die. She will live for ever. She will always be with me, everywhere. She is with me. She is with me as I walk and talk. She is with me as I eat and sleep. She is in the breeze that softly hisses through the leaves of the trees, in the wind that I breathe, in the rain that soothes my body after a hot day, in the night that accompanies my sleep. She lives in my memories of her, reigns in them, like a queen, supreme, black, beautiful, proud and strong.

I know there are things in life that one cannot help. The weight of years necessarily took its toll on Mema. That's how life is. Things must come and go. Trees grow tall, then one day the wind blows them down. A river springs from the bosom of the earth and nourishes the lives of the fishes, then it dries out, taking away the lives it had created. It is in the nature of things that the years should take their toll. But the years did not vanquish Mema, because Mema was strong, a strong woman indeed.

Mema had a big mouth too. And when I say a big mouth, I mean she really had a big mouth. Not in the physical sense. But in the sense of the things she said, and how she said them. Somewhere in her heart, Mema always believed she was the most intelligent person in the universe. It was not easy to win a debate against her. She would always try to convince others that she was right. But she was never easily convinced. I vaguely remember those times when she would have a dispute with either her husband, my father, or other people in the village. The days following the dispute would always be days filled with tension. They would also be days of apparent hatred during which Mema would adopt a stubborn demeanour, working her way silently throughout the hut and the village. She would not speak to anyone and nobody would dare to speak to her. When she was in such a mood, even my father could not dare to approach her. I have never been able to tell whether this was part of my mother's theatrical way of doing things, or whether she was serious. All I can tell is that this could go on for days.

Of course, as was required by our village customs, when a member of the community was at odds with another, someone from among the most influential speakers in the village had to attempt a reconciliation. It did not matter whether the dispute was a private matter between husband and wife, or a public matter between two villagers. Something had to be done. But the task of reconciling estranged parties was particularly daunting when Mema was involved. The person secretly appointed by the village to act as mediator would have to approach her with extreme caution and expert tact, for fear of my mother's mouth. Everybody knew her mouth. Everybody knew that her mouth could become a terrible weapon if caused to start spitting out words like bullets.

So, my mother would sit there, patiently listening to the village mediator. Reassured, the mediator would continue his speech of appeasement, encouraged by my mother's apparent willingness to listen. But, as could be expected, my mother would eventually interrupt:

'Have you finished?'

Startled, the speaker would say:

'Errrr . . . yes. I mean . . . Not really . . . You know . . . I . . .'

'Because if you have finished,' my mother's mouth would strike, 'let me tell you one thing . . .'

And my mother's mouth would start to talk. It would talk longer and longer, bigger and bigger, and louder and louder, with that high-pitched something that always caused the insides of people to shrink, you know, the kind of thing that happens to your insides when you are afraid. The kind of thing that made you want to rush out to pee in the bushes behind the hut, only to find out that you did not have anything to pee out at all. Yes, that's it. Fear. Fright. That is what people experienced when my mother's mouth started to talk. She had the kind of strong voice that could be heard from one village corner to the other. When that voice started to talk, it sounded very frightful to both males and females.

Was my mother angry about something? Perhaps. About what? I cannot tell. All I remember is that when that voice came out of a mouth that was going to spit out feelings of anger, spite, sorrow and sadness, it was unstoppable. It really caused heavy shrinking in your bowels. And when that voice was heard thundering into the air like thousands of guns, the village would stop breathing for a while. They just knew. It was her again.

Gathering his courage with both of his hands, the mediator would try to continue:

'Woman . . . Please listen to me a bit. I am just trying to . . .'

'Woman what?' my mother would interrupt. 'Did you hear me talking when you were telling me your nonsense? No! Now I say: listen to my side of the story, and after that, go and tell that animal what I have told you here today, do you hear me well?'

And my mother would start to talk. She would talk for hours, for days and for months. She would spit words out like bombs, burning the village with their atrocious fire. Her words would rush out like troops on the assault and invade the village, taking no prisoners. They would tornado over the village like a hurricane, blowing off thatch rooftops. She would drown the village in the mortal lake of her words, hammering them like a carpenter his nails, leaving of her victims only lifeless ant-gnawed carcasses that told of her memorable passage. Tired of listening to this indomitable woman, the mediator would simply walk out, vanquished and swearing never again, in the future, to accept a mediation involving this woman.

My mother was a good speaker. Like all the village people who mastered the art of speech, she always began her talks with a tale or a proverb that was appropriate for the particular situation. And since my mother had a tale or a proverb for all the situations in which she was involved, I believe she herself was a treasure trove of tales and proverbs.

In my village, good speakers had a tale for every situation. You could not claim to be a good speaker if you knew no tale. In the days of my childhood, tales were like the water with which you helped the rebellious food down your throat. They still are, but in my village only, perhaps. Things have changed so much in our land since my childhood. So, I cannot be certain that what I am saying here is still true. But that is how I remember the things of my childhood. Yes, I remember. I remember that whenever there was a problem that needed community intervention or decision, some *medzo* were held in the *aba* judiciously situated at the centre of the village. I liked the village *medzo* because, for me, they were not just about trying difficult cases. They were also a learning experience. They were the ideal place to be for a child who wanted to acquire the wisdom of the elders. A wisdom made of tales and proverbs, of wise decisions taken in order to ensure peace among village members. Tales told during village *medzo* were always full of dreams of better worlds. That is why I liked them so much. They were full of life, of fantasy lands, of worlds known and unknown, of past memories, of myths and stories long forgotten. They were always full of evil acts and good deeds, of long-fought epic battles lost and won, of challenges and rewards, of heroes and villains, of victories and defeats, of lives ended and begun. They were life itself and they brought wisdom to both the speaker and the listener. Through tales, the speakers acquired the wisdom to make a good speech that would inspire the community's decisions. Through tales, the listeners acquired the wisdom that would enable them to learn about the tribulations of life and how to cope with them.

In my village, elders never gave direct advice to youngsters. When a youngster approached an elder with the words 'Father' or 'Mother, I have a problem. Teach me how to cope with it,' the elder would say: 'Sit here, my son' or 'Sit here, my daughter.' This 'Sit here' was then followed by a 'Let me tell you a story.' Thus, the elder would begin to tell a well-chosen tale that would impart wisdom. After telling the tale, the elder would not say 'Do this' or 'Do that'. Instead, he or she would simply get up and go, leaving the youngsters alone to ponder over the meaning of the story. It was up to the youngsters to show cleverness by getting out of the tale the wisdom that they needed.

Village *medzo* were like that too. They were about bringing wisdom to the behaviour of people. Tales made them like that. Village *medzo* would be boring without tales. In my village, and in all other villages of the area and beyond, tales were what made people wise. No man or woman was considered wise without the mastery of tales and proverbs. The more you knew, the wiser you were thought to be, and my people always called upon the wisest elders when there were cases to try.

So, village *medzo* were never boring. They were vibrant. They were battlegrounds where wisdoms confronted other wisdoms. I remember some *medzo* that would cause two villages to gather. Two villages gathering because of *medzo* was always a crucial moment, tense with all sorts of emotions. Two villages could be holding *medzo* in preparation for a happy event such as a marriage. But at times there were *medzo* filled with hardened emotions such as anger or even hatred. Village *medzo* were never a casual affair. Often, two villages gathering because of *medzo* meant that something had gone seriously wrong between them.

The most common *medzo* that would cause two villages to gather related to unhealthy marriages. Most of the time, the story would be the same. A woman had been savagely beaten by her husband, or so she claimed. Another woman had fled the village because her in-laws did not like her and had been treating her like a dog since she became a spouse to this village three years ago. Or so she claimed. And since she had not been happy, the woman had fled from her husband's family to return to her parents in her own native village. Such an occurrence was always viewed as a curse. 'Not again!' the villagers would exclaim. 'Not again!' They now knew that in one way or the other, one of the villages, the faulty one, would have to pay a heavy price. Of course, that price would almost always be paid by the husband's village.

As could be expected, the wife's relatives would always issue a blackmail statement. The statement would threaten the husband and his people, informing them that their wife was now in the custody of her people, that she had told them the whole truth about how she had been treated and that she was not returning to her in-laws' village. However, because this was the first offence, they were ready to listen to the remedies the husband's people were going to propose. But, more than anything else, the sufferings lacerating their hurt hearts had to be soothed. Their daughter was therefore not going to return to her husband unless something was done to alleviate the pain they felt when their daughter came crying to them. The angry husband, of course, would pretend not to care. He would argue, with pride, that he was not going to lower himself into going to beg for a woman who had disgraced him. Without consulting his people, he would send his in-laws an inflammatory statement telling them that he was coming to soothe nobody's heart and that they could keep their daughter as long as they wanted.

Such statements always marked the beginning of psychological games and scare tactics. The days following the woman's flight would always be days of observation and silence. Every evening and every afternoon after work in the fields, the husband's people would start to sit in the *aba* more than they usually did. Those who rarely came to the *aba* would start to visit it more often than usual. They would sit there in silence, or kill time playing their favourite game of *songo*. Some would go to the *aba* just to watch the road along which the woman had fled. They knew that at times, overwhelmed by the love she felt for her husband and by the absence caused by the separation, a woman could unexpectedly decide to come back to him, thus saving the village from undertaking a painful process of recovery. It had been seen before, had it not? So, sometimes a woman would indeed lose patience upon seeing that her husband was not coming to claim her back as quickly as she had hoped. As days and months passed without any sign from her husband, the woman would be gripped by a frenzied unrest that did not sit well with her own parents and relatives. It was disgraceful, they would say, trying to convince her, for a woman who had fled from her husband to return to the same man without first making him come to beg for her. An arrogant husband who dared to ridicule his in-laws deserved the most severe punishment for his crimes against their daughter, above all when such crimes risked bringing shame on all those who carried the same blood as herself. Was it not the utmost form of disrespect for a man not to come to his in-laws to beg for his wife? Did this not show he valued goat shit more than he valued his in-laws? 'Shame!' They would say. 'Shame!'

'And this was the same man who had used the stratagem of *abom* to force the people of this village to agree to give him their daughter in marriage? Did he not come to this village at night to kidnap his future wife in defiance of her people? Whoever gave our people the idea of allowing this custom to thrive? Now you see. When a man who knows the people of the woman he wants may not allow him to marry her uses *abom* to steal her from her village, nothing good can come out of it. And our daughters are really foolish to agree to being kidnapped this way. A respectful daughter should always consult her elders before doing something like this. By making herself the accomplice of her future husband, does she not, by this very fact, bring humiliation to her village? Think about it. Nothing is more humiliating than a village receiving a message one day that their daughter has been kidnapped by her suitor, and that she would not be returned to her people unless they agreed to her marriage with her kidnapper. A bad custom indeed. A terrible custom. A custom such as *abom*, that allows the daughter of a village to partake in the humiliation of her own people by running away with her kidnapper, is no good. A custom that allows a daughter to force her people to agree to a marriage, simply because she loves a man that she thinks her people will reject, is an abomination. And now you see. The shame is upon us again. So now we say enough. Our daughter will not be going back to that man in this shameful manner. Are past humiliations not enough?'

This man had treated them like goat shit. For this reason, they argued, their daughter could not go back, unless she really wanted to bring unbearable shame upon her people. But the woman could no longer wait. Shame? Well, what else could she do? She loved her husband too much. And she did not want him to go and get himself another wife. She really had to go. So, in the end, vanquished by the impatient tension that now tortured her mercilessly, and unable to wait any longer, she would suddenly decide to ignore her parents' advice and go back to her husband. She would give as reasons the facts that, on the one hand, it was going to be planting season soon and she did not want to lose the possibility of good crops next year, and that, on the other hand, she had left her children behind and they were probably very unhappy without her.

The husband's people knew this could happen. They knew it was a rare occurrence for a woman simply to decide to return to her man in such a dishonourable manner, but they were comforted by the fact that some women had done it. If it had happened before, there was no reason why it should not happen again. So, they secretly sang their prayers to the gods and spirits, invoked their ancestors and waited in hope. When this did not work, they would consult some *minguegan* who possessed the power of seeing both the past and the future. The *nguegan* summoned by the villagers would hold a divination ceremony during which he would consult the spirits of his clan. He would wear his *nguegan* garments and paint his face white with a substance that, in the dim light of the oil lamps, made him appear as frightening as a ghost. He would utter frightful unintelligible sounds, throw himself to the ground, roll in the mud and suddenly stand erect on his feet, immobile and silent. He would rush into the crowd, causing panic among the audience. At times, his speech would become normal and he would be heard calling on the spirits. 'Spirits and gods of our people,' he would say, 'show me the light. Show me the truth. I have eaten the powder from the sacred bones of my clan's totems, I have swallowed the venom of the sacred snake, I have cleansed myself according to the rules taught me by my dead grandfather.

Now, I am asking you to show me the truth. And I am asking you: is she coming or not?' Then, as if suddenly exhausted by all the activity, he would return to his seat, and fall asleep. He would snore like a troop of elephants. A few hours later, he would wake up and say to the audience: 'During my sleep, I travelled to the land of the spirits. This is what they said . . .' And he would inform the village of the decision of the spirits. Whether good or bad, the *nguegan*'s verdict would still not be sufficient to appease the villagers.

So, the husband's people would keep coming to the *aba* every day, hoping to witness personally the miracle return. They would keep their gaze glued to the road on which the woman had escaped. They knew she would have to re-enter the village from that same direction. They would stay in the *aba* until very late in the night, and would even post vigils there at night to keep watch. They knew the miracle had occurred when the recognizable shadow of the returning woman was spotted trying to enter the village in the middle of the night. The villagers would breathe a big sigh of relief and silently cry victory. One by one, husbands sitting in the *aba* would happily run back home to tell their wives. And their wives would run to their best friends' huts and gossip about a return that, contrary to the men, they thought was a shameful one, a return that, according to them, was casting a bad image on other women. The news would spread and soon would be known by all.

The next day, the women of the village would suddenly remember that the returning wife's yard had the best vegetables in the village. They really needed some for their evening meals. So would begin a strange parade of women trying to be first to get the best glimpse of their unfortunate colleague. While pretending to be innocent passers-by, they would risk an eye through the open front door of her kitchen hut. Unable to see anything, they would strain their ears, hoping to catch a volatile sound. Unable to wait any longer, some would take their courage with both hands and enter the kitchen. There, the women would stand in silence. On their cheeks would flow the tears of the unspeakable sadness that now gripped them. Together, they would mourn, cursing those evil men who had no honour left in them and who would go to great lengths to ridicule their wives.

◆

But this was just one possible version of the story. Women did not always return. In fact, more often than not, days would pass, followed by months, and no womanly shadow would be seen surreptitiously entering the village at night. Then a strange unrest would start to grip the husband and his people. They knew that the longer the separation, the harder it would be to get the woman back without paying a heavier fine. The husband would start to spend restless nights thinking about how he was going to get his wife back. He would start to curse his pride. He would also curse himself for having let the woman go in the first place. Several burning months would thus go by, and still no woman would be seen stealing into the village at night. So, each passing day and night would become a sleepless hell for the men and women of the offending village. They would feel as if they had been sleeping on a bed of burning charcoal. Then, something strange would start to happen in the village. The spirits who guarded over sleep would start to hear whispering voices seething through from each hut. These voices would start as feebly as the whisper of the wind caressing the thatch roofs of the huts with its invisible hand. Then, as the nights went by, the voices would grow stronger and stronger, louder and louder. The wind would soon harden its hand over the roofs, now seeking to destroy them with its impatient breath.

'Ah Yosep?' The question was put in the inquisitive voice of a woman. There was no doubt it was coming from the main hut of Yosep's household.

'Mmmh . . .'

'Are you sleeping?'

'Mmmh . . .' The 'mmmh' was reluctantly uttered by the male body that was sleeping by the inquisitive woman. This reluctant 'mmmh' meant that the body knew what was coming next.

'Tell me one thing, Yosep,' the woman's voice would continue. 'I have a question that has been haunting me for a while. And since you are not sleeping, I need to know your thought about it. Do you love me?'

'This woman. Can you not let a man sleep without asking him such questions in the middle of the night?'

'Ah! You want to sleep! I have asked you a simple question. A question that requires a very simple answer. Yes or no. And what do you say? "I want to sleep"!'

'Woman, please. I do not want to argue with you. You know that nighttime is no time for arguments. Do you know how many ears, some good, some evil, are straining themselves to hear our conversation? Can't you wait until tomorrow when it is daytime?'

'Yosep!' interrupted the woman's voice. 'Look at my face. Is it written with charcoal here that I am an idiot?'

'No . . . But . . . I mean . . .'

'Then, why do you think I am a child? Do you think you can lie to me as one would to a child whose question one would prefer not to answer? I have said: "Do you love me?" And what do you do? You insult me by treating me like an idiot. I will not speak to you any more. I will not speak to you until you have answered my question, I swear. My ancestors are my witnesses.'

And so would fall upon the village a period of doomed silence when wives would not want to speak to their husbands. Worse

15

still, at night wives would turn their backs to their men or simply leave the conjugal bed to sleep on the mat on the bedroom floor. Food would still be cooked, but the reluctant expression on the women's faces foretold nothing good. In one house, a wife would neglectfully thrust plates at her husband's feet, almost knocking the food over. In another, a woman would stubbornly refuse to go to the spring to fetch water for her husband's ablutions. Even farm work would suffer. Women would be spotted holding secret meetings in their peanut fields, and they would return home in the afternoon after doing no work at all. The men knew war had been declared upon them, and there was simply no way they were going to win that war.

'Ah Akoma, my beloved wife, since when do you serve me food without water?'

'Ah! You think I am your slave? I do not remember my father telling you, when you paid the marriage *n'sua* to my people fifteen *mimbuh* ago, that he had sold me to you as a slave. If you want water to drink, go and get your water yourself. Don't you have two legs like me? Besides, you are sitting closer to the water pot than I am.'

Faced with this womanly assault, the man would simply shut up and look, speechless and overwhelmed, at this woman of his who had obviously elected to turn his life into a living hell. Night would come again, and from hut to hut, the same questions would be asked over and over again.

'Ah Nkulanveng, my husband. I have a question for you, and I need an answer now. Do you really love me?'

'Of course, my wife, I love you. Isn't that what I told you the day when I saw you for the first time?'

'Yes, I remember. I remember that you were a constant visitor to my village because you had friends there with whom you used to go monkey-hunting.'

16

'*Owé*. But monkey-hunting was just a pretext that allowed me to see you as often as I could. But I had to be careful not to approach you openly, because at that time a young man and a young woman were not allowed to see each other secretly or even to talk openly to each other without the presence of elders. All I could do was to watch you from afar and let my heart throb frantically in my chest because of the love it felt for you.'

'So you took advantage of the fact that you and I had the chance to meet during the wrestling contest that was held in your village. You lured me away from my parents who were too busy watching the sweating wrestlers to pay attention to what I was doing. You lured me into following you behind a hut.'

'*Owé*. And it was there that I told you that I loved you for the first time.'

'*Owé*. I remember. I remember the joy I felt and the throbs my heart gave me when you told me this. I told you that I loved you too.'

'And I said: "If it is true that your heart is throbbing for me, then I will come to visit you in your village. Do you agree?"'

'"I agree," was my answer. After our secret encounter, I heard the cock crow three times one morning after the other, and there you were with your people. You had come to ask me to leave my parents and become one of yours. Two full moons later, I moved into your village to become your wife.'

'Those were good times.'

'*Owé*. Good times, indeed. But what I am asking you now is this: do you really love me? Do you still love me the way you said you loved me during that day when we met behind the hut and exchanged words of love for the first time?'

'My ancestors are my witnesses that I still love you so.'

'If you love me like you say, why have you not told all the husbands of this village to go and fetch Ntutume's wife? It has now been moons almost as many as the fingers on both of my hands, and no one has budged a finger to go and get her back. Is that the way you show your love for me?'

'But, woman . . . Biloghe is not my wife. If it were you who had gone, you know I would have got you back very quickly.'

'Nonsense! When did family problems become one man's problems in this village? You know perfectly well that it is everybody's duty in this village to go and try to get Ntutume's wife back from her people.'

'You are right, woman, but . . .'

'There is no "but". Why do you insist on insulting me? You just said you loved me, did you not? The question is: would you have waited this long before coming to my village to beg me back?'

'No . . . but . . .'

'What I see is that all the males in this village have been very silent and inactive since Biloghe left. No one, so far, has tried to get the village to go and beg her back. So, do not lie to me. This is exactly what you would have done if it were me who had left. You would have made no attempt to go and beg me back. Is this how you do things in this village? Is this the way you show love for your women in this place?'

'Woman mine, it is not I who will say that what you have said is not true. I understand what you are saying. Let me think about it.'

'Owé. You had better think about it fast. For I have had enough of your nonsense. So, today I will say this, and my dead people are my witnesses: think about it before I decide that it is also time for me to leave this village. Do something before we, women of this village, decide that it is not worthwhile staying in a village such as this one that does not care enough about the wives it marries.'

18

From hut to hut, the same threat would be repeated, and a silence as thick as the skin of an elephant would fall upon the village. This new menace from the women would reverberate through the air, seethe through the openings of the mud-walled huts and instil deep apprehension in the hearts of the men. They had all gone through the same ordeal with their wives at night. They had been unable to have a good night's sleep for a long while and they knew they would continue to be kept awake for many more nights to come. They also knew not only from experience, but also from their mothers, that when a woman was angry, nothing worked in the village. A woman would starve a whole village to death when she was angry. Thus, the men understood that the time had come for a recovery action to be undertaken. Little by little, men would start to talk to one another. And the groups of two or three would soon grow into groups of ten, and the groups of ten would become bigger groups. In the end, a session of village *medzo* would become unavoidable. The elders of the village would summon everyone to the *aba* so that the *medzo* regarding the departure of Biloghe could be discussed, and an appropriate action undertaken. Something had to be done. Urgently.

Some two or three mornings later, a messenger would be sent to Biloghe's village to announce the forthcoming arrival of Ntutume's people. He would specify that Ntutume and his people were coming to have a courtesy chat with their in-laws because they had not had one for a very long time. And it was vital to the preservation of good in-law relations that such chats be held from time to time to ensure that no one had anything against the other. So, on the announced day, Ntutume's people would set off to Biloghe's village to beg her back. Because they were the primary parties to this issue, neither Ntutume nor Biloghe would be allowed to open their mouths during the *medzo*. Their people would do the talking for them. They would speak only if specifically asked to do so by one of the elders handling the arguments.

'We know we have offended you,' the head speaker from Ntutume's village would say to their in-laws. 'That is why we have asked for this meeting between our two villages. Our forefathers used to say that he is a fool who does not know how to beg. We have come to beg for the return of our wife. We therefore thank you for agreeing to this *medzo* because it will allow all of us to know what caused two of our children to part, and how to prevent this from happening again. It is clear that we cannot let this situation persist. By giving us your daughter, you agreed that our two villages should become united not only through the bloods of our two married children, but also through the bloods of the children to whom they have given birth. Nothing can break the blood ties that now unite our villages. Yet, how can we live in peace knowing that our daughter and wife has left us, and that the children that she accepted to bear for us are claiming her back?'

An elder from Biloghe's village stood up to speak.

'We have heard your words, man. And your words are wise. But as wise as they may be, how can they erase the sorrow that has befallen us since our daughter came back to us crying almost ten moons ago? Ten moons! I do not remember ever seeing a daughter staying this long away from her loving family without such a family coming to make sure that their daughter has been healthy all this time. Doesn't a hand that loses one of its fingers become awkward? Did your hand not feel awkward after it lost one of its fingers ten moons ago? Such is the question that I am asking you.'

'We have heard your angry words, father of our wife. We have heard and we are therefore crying before you like a child who has been beaten by his father. Like such a child, we are

20

crying and begging for forgiveness. But is it because our father has beaten us that we must turn around and run away?'

The speaker from Ntutume's village paused. He looked around him, contemplating and trying to read the faces that were staring at him from the audience. He was expecting an answer from them.

'No!' came the answer in unison.

'No,' continued the speaker, reassured. 'It is not because a father beats his son that the son must turn around and run away from his father. A father never beats his children unless they have done something terribly wrong. A child raised to be a responsible person knows this very well. So he must accept his punishment because he knows his father loves him. He must therefore come back home after hiding in the forest to cry off his sorrow.'

'*Owé*. That is the way it should be!' the audience responded.

'Ya! So if that is the way it should be, why should our father deny us the right to come back to him to beg for forgiveness?'

'He should not!' the crowd roared.

'Good. So the question we are asking our father is the following: do you want us back into your hut? I have spoken.'

A murmur of appreciation ran through the crowd. Nkulanveng had always been a good speaker. He was feared in this area for the way in which he was able to use his tongue and knowledge of customs and words to win a debate for his people. During the *medzo* he had been appointed to handle as lead speaker, he was always able to twist words inside his mouth like lianas. With these, he would tie hard knots around the tongues of his opponents, who would suddenly appear clumsy in their speech. Nkulanveng was a speech master who knew how to make every word beautiful and convincing, and the crowds always drank his wisdom like water on a hot day. In such *medzo* assemblies as this one, Nkulanveng's art of speech was especially appreciated because he was always able to save his village from the most entangled situations. When village honour was at stake, Nkulanveng was the person who could obtain appropriate compensation from the offending village. So, whenever he started to speak, everyone would listen very intently, drinking his wise words like fresh water just fetched from a spring in the forest mountains nearby.

Today's *medzo* were no different. Nkulanveng had spoken. It was now up to someone from the in-law village to break Nkulanveng's spell by picking up the challenge that had been laid down before them.

The crowd waited in silence. Tension was building up in the air as faces stared straight into the eyes of other faces and heads turned left and right waiting for someone to undo the web that Nkulanveng had just woven. Suddenly, a throat cleared from behind the crowd. Someone wished to speak. People stepped aside to clear the view towards this person. An old woman from Biloghe's village painstakingly stood up on two bony legs that seemed to bend under the weight of her frail body. The whole structure of her body was supported by a walking cane that seemed to be the only thing that was preventing those legs from breaking. It was Meleng, Biloghe's grandmother from her mother's side. Meleng happened to be in the village on a family visit. She had come from her own village one moon before, and was preparing to leave when the *medzo* were announced. She decided to stay a few more days to see how the *medzo* were going to go. Meleng was a frequent visitor to Biloghe's village because her daughter, who was Biloghe's mother, was a wife of this village. These visits were important to her because she liked to make sure her daughter and grandchildren were all right. Because of her illnesses that were becoming more and more insistent due to her age, she had not recently been able to come and visit them as frequently as she used to. She had therefore not seen them for a while. This visit, she sensed, could be the last before she joined her ancestors. So, she wanted to see her grandchildren one last time before being called off to the world of the dead.

'Héééééééé!' she started in a thin, shaky voice, slowly clapping her hands five times to mark her amazement. The clapping almost caused her to tumble to the floor because she had taken the cane off the ground in order to clap with both of her hands. She quickly returned the cane to the ground to keep her balance.

'Today's children,' she continued, 'today's children are funny. Nowadays children think that they are cleverer than their elders. So they boast publicly about their intelligence and their sharp tongues. Of course, my son who has just spoken has shown that he comes from a good family, and a good village. His people should be proud of him because he is of the race of people who are born to lead others. Yet, he is only a child in the eyes of someone like me who has wiped the buttocks of many children and grandchildren. So I will not blame him for being clever.'

Old Meleng paused a moment, clearing her throat while assessing the reaction of the crowd that was now hanging on her lips and wondering what kind of counter-attack she was going to come up with.

'I have said that the child who has just spoken is clever, but can his cleverness, his understanding of matters such as these *medzo*, be superior to the knowledge of those who wiped his buttocks? The child asked an interesting question. He asked whether or not his father wished him back into his hut. I do not blame him for that because that is the sort of question that a child who has offended his father should always ask. But he forgot to mention one thing. When a child runs away from his father after offending him, he must return home immediately after crying off his pain. By coming back home shortly after his punishment, he is showing his father that he has understood, and his father is thus prepared to give him his blessing. But if the child runs and stays away one moon after another, showing no sign of regret, the father may consider this a more serious offence because the child is clearly saying to him that he is not coming back to get the blessings of his father. The father may thus forget him and never forgive.'

Meleng was interrupted by a fit of dry coughing that caused her to struggle with her throat for a while. She managed to clear her voice and resume her speech.

'So, what I am saying is that a child who stays away is in fact telling his father that he does not want to come back, and that he does not want to beg for forgiveness. Such a child can only be a lost child to the offended father. But because a child is only a child, he often discovers that no place is like home. Our forefathers and their forefathers before them used to say this: you can say that the person over there was my wife, but you can never say that the person standing over there was my brother, my mother or my father. No. You cannot say so because someone who is linked to you by blood cannot get rid of that blood. Two brothers born from the same mother cannot suddenly declare: "We were never born from the same *ébón*." That is impossible. Have I said well, my people?'

'*Ekééééé! Owé!* You have said well, mother,' the crowd shouted.

'Ya! So what I am saying to the boy who has just spoken and to our visitors is that it is they who have offended their father. I do not like the question that was asked. They asked their father whether he still wants them back in his hut. That question turns things around. It puts the blame on the father instead of putting it on the son. It makes the father feel guilty for an offence that the son committed against him. When have you ever seen

24

someone coming to beg for forgiveness and at the same time putting the blame on that very person that he offended?'

'Never!' the audience reacted in agreement.

'So let me therefore turn the question around and hand it back to our visitors. Let the father answer his son's question with a question. Does our son still want to come back to the home of his father? Also, does he know how much I have suffered from his absence? Does he know how much I have cried because of his absence? Does he know how angry I am with him for deciding not to come back home earlier to beg for my blessings? I have finished!'

The old woman returned painfully to her seat, helped by young people. A roar of voices saluted her last words. 'Ah! These old women . . . No one can be cleverer than they are. Where did they learn all these tricks of knowledge? Well, you know, never play with those old people. After all, didn't they give birth to us? Yes? So why do you expect younger people to surpass them in wit?'

The brouhaha from the amazed voices of the excited crowd eventually died down. Nkulanveng stood up again. His riddle had been undone by old Meleng. He knew he could not afford to offer her another opening. After all, they were here to get Biloghe back. All considerations had to be subjected to that imperative. His pride had to be set aside, above all because he had been vanquished, not by a peer, but by an old mother who still had a lot of things to teach people of his generation.

'We have heard you, mother,' Nkulanveng began. 'Wisdom has spoken through your mouth and we all know wisdom is sacred. What else can a disobedient child do when his father has shown such a profound grief? Let me and my people go and chat a little bit.'

The people from Ntutume's village stood up and disappeared

behind a hut. They took the time that it takes for a man suffering from diarrhoea to go and satisfy his needs in the bushes. When they came back from their consultations, Nkulanveng greeted his in-laws again.

'Fathers and mothers of Abang, *ma veh mine mbolo!*'

'*Mbolo!*' the people of Abang greeted back.

'Are your ears listening?' Nkulanveng asked.

'*Owé.* We are listening. Speak, son of Abasok. Speak and share your wisdom with us.'

'Fathers and mothers of Biloghe, let me tell you something that has been troubling my heart since the time my wife left me. I have thought a lot. I have thought a long time. But do you know what made me suffer most? The unbearable idea that I may have offended you. I have agonized day and night over the terrible thought that I may not have shown you the respect that is due to you. I know that I should not have waited this long to come and ask for your forgiveness. I should have come straight away to ask for your blessings. But you know from experience how a child who is afraid of his father often reacts. He hesitates, fearing that his father will not even want to listen to his pleas. But, today, we have braved our fears to appear before you at last. Isn't that the most important thing? We have come to beg back our daughter and wife. And we are doing so openly. Is there any shame in begging for what you have lost in foolishness?'

'No, there is none!' the crowd agreed.

'Is it shameful for a man to go to his in-laws and beg for his wife when he can no longer live without her?'

'No, it is not!'

'Is there anything shameful in going to your in-laws to say: fathers and mothers of my wife, I want the mother of my children back because our children are missing her?'

'No, there is none at all!' the crowd concluded in unison.

'So, today I am saying to my in-laws who are sitting here that the same blood that runs through their veins also runs through the veins of the children that their daughter gave me. Our blood is the same because it has mixed in the bodies of our children to become one. He who says that the children belong to the man alone is a fool. Don't children often run to their mother's relatives when things are not going well with their father's people? And when the children have grown up, who can prevent them from going to live in their mother's land? We have acknowledged our wrongs, that is why we have come. We are begging for forgiveness.'

'Yes, we are, truly,' answered Nkulanveng's people. Reassured, the speaker continued:

'So, in order to soothe your hurt hearts, please accept these fifty domjons of *malamba* beer that our children brewed with the best sugar canes in our village. They will quench the thirst and burning that the sorrow has caused in your throats. Accept these ten pieces of cloth that will wipe your tears away. We have also brought you five goats, eight cocks and twenty hens whose presence will always remind you of the fact that we came here today to strengthen our family ties.'

Biloghe's mother stood up.

'*Mbolo, ah be minki*,' she said, greeting her in-laws. 'I know that I should not stand to speak at such a crucial time. Our custom has always made it clear that people of my age who are direct parties to a *medzo* should not speak in serious matters such as this one. It has made it the domain of the elders alone, because the concerned parties, above all when they are couples or young, often tend to spoil the broth if left to express themselves directly. The wisdom of the elders has always spared our people the kinds of troubles that young people are capable of causing. I do not have anything against this custom, because I believe it is a wise custom. However, I also know that no woman or man was ever killed for daring to speak where the custom said they could not. Besides, I am the mother of that very woman who was beaten in her body and humiliated in her soul by that man sitting over there. So, I will speak. I will say to my son sitting over there –' she pointed at Ntutume, Biloghe's husband – 'I will say to him that when I gave him my child, I did not say to him, "Take her. I have sold her to you and you can do whatever you want with her." No. That is not what I said. I said to him, "Here is my child. I am giving her to you so that you can take good care of her as your wife." I know that a husband may sometimes get angry and beat his wife, but who declared that this should become a custom of our land? People have told me how, after getting drunk with your *malamba*, you would get back home and beat my daughter up for no reason. Is that the way your people tell you a man should behave? No! So, I am asking you all who are sitting here today: does a man show he is strong by beating his wife for no reason?'

'No! Such a man is a coward!' roared the crowd.

'So, hear me well this time, my son. I do not hate you and I forgive you. But I say, let me not hear again that you have put your hands on my child and beaten her for no reason. Show your strength with other men, and leave my daughter alone. When you leave our village today, she will go with you. I give her to you today just like I did when you first came here to ask for her. You gave us her *n'sua* as is required by our customs and I said, "Take care of her." Now, that's what I am saying again. Take good care of her. I can pay you back your *n'sua* at any time, but will you be able to give me back my daughter if she dies in your hands as a result of your brutality? So, I will repeat my warning: let me not hear that you have mistreated her again. I have finished!'

A thoughtful silence followed this speech by Biloghe's mother. Everyone understood the significance of her words. She had spoken the mere truth. An *n'sua* can always be returned to a husband who decides to separate himself from his wife, but once someone has been killed, that person is lost for ever. No *n'sua* can ever be sufficient to pay for someone's life.

The *medzo* thus ended on this poignant motherly note. As the two communities parted that day, everyone went away pondering over the words of Biloghe's mother, words that symbolized the respect that men and women used to show one another in our villages in times long gone.

My mother's story is a sad one. It is a story that should not be told. It should be left untold, lost in the sacred secrecy of long-held memories whose tabooness should have helped to keep them secret and unprofaned for ever. So why am I telling this story? Why am I profaning memories that should not be profaned, memories meant to die with the world itself? Where did I find the courage even to think of telling a story as atrocious as this one? Is it a sign of the times that I should defy my fear of the taboo and venture into profaning my memories of my mother, memories that are also her own, memories made of stories told me at various times of my short life with her? Is it because I have travelled across the seas to the white man's land that I have decided to desecrate my mother's memories by telling them to strangers who will not even care to read her story to the end? Strangers who may not like what I have to say or may hate me for daring to say it? And how could strangers understand what I have to say? What will they do when the story of my mother proves too much for them and starts to haunt them, eating them from the inside? And what about the spirits of the ancestors of my land? Will they be happy? I know they are watching. They are watching and frowning at me in desperate disapproval.

Sacrilege! Blasphemy! I can hear the accusations. I can feel them. They are like spines in my throat. Sharp spines all over my body, lacerating my flesh with a thousand wounds. It is a torture. The torture is unbearable. I hear the wind blowing with anger around me. The spirits of my people are unsettled. They demand that I stop. They cannot allow me to continue. The rain has started to fall over my house. The spirits are crying. They know I am not going to stop. I can't. I must tell this story. The urge to tell is stronger than my will. The thunder is growling over my head. The lightning is trying to blind my eyes. It is trying to burn them, to stop me from seeing what I am writing. The universe is angry with me. The trees and the wind are plotting against me. What are they plotting? Revenge? Retribution? For what? Against whom? Blasphemy! Betrayal! Something is being profaned. The spirits are shaken. Horrified. They are speaking. They are speaking a language I cannot understand. They are speaking in a tongue that sounds like my own, yet I cannot understand what they are saying. Their mouths are uttering words and those words are taking a life of their own. They want to torture me. They want to destroy my mind and stop the profanation. The words are hissing around me like snakes. They are made of rings as thick as those of a boa constrictor, a boa growing thicker and thicker before my very eyes. And now the boa has opened wide its mouth, ready to swallow me whole. I want to fight but I cannot. The words are many boas, and the boas are my prison. They are all dancing and turning around me, becoming ungraspable and invisible as they clash against one another. I can hear them hissing furiously but I cannot see them any more. The invisible tom-tom to whose silent sounds they were dancing has stopped. But the hissing continues. I can still hear the voices. There! I just saw a ghost flying through the house. It was brought here by the lightning. A warning? The ghost had the face of my ancestors. I could see all their faces in the face of the ghost. It was one face in many faces. Or many faces in one face. I am not sure. My nights are nightmares. I cannot sleep. My eyes are burning me. My hands are refusing to obey me. They are hurting. My head is hurting.

My bowels are hurting. I am burning inside. But I must sit. I must continue the story. The story wants to remain untold. Unprofaned. Because it is not a tellable story. It is a story that wants to die and be forgotten. But I cannot forget. I cannot afford to forget.

I must remember.

I remember.

Mema.

Mother.

My mother.

That mother of mine was herself a strong believer in things that should not be profaned, in things that should go unquestioned because they were truths that were self-evident and manifest in our surroundings. She was very deeply rooted in the belief that things always happened for a reason, and that there would always be truths beyond the perception and grasp of humans.

Mema, I hear, was so unlike my father. Pepa. My father. Who was he really? I do not know. I did not really know my father. He joined the ancestors long before I became fully aware of the things happening around me. So I have but a faint memory of what he could have been like. All I know of him is what Mema and other people told me. The story went that Pepa was a very calm and placid man with no real manly power in our household. My mother, her critics said, ran every single thing in the hut with a heavy hand, and a big mouth. Pepa, I was told, had been turned into a mere woman in his own hut. He had become an empty shell. A soundless tom-tom. A lion with broken legs who could no longer bounce and pounce. He was thought of as someone so subdued and bewildered by the power wielded by his wife inside and outside the hut that his voice was never heard rising above that of the panther of a woman that people called his wife. This was not normal, people said. This woman must have used witchcraft to subdue her husband. It was customary, they said, for women to use witchcraft to control their husbands' will in order to prevent them from looking at other women or marrying themselves a second wife. They would, for example, put strange things in their foods and under the conjugal bed. These things would then slowly take over the manhood and will of the husband, who would become very docile. If the husband dared to go to another woman, his manhood would refuse to stand up to perform its duties. It would stand only when used with the woman who controlled it with witchcraft. So, according to the gossip, there was no doubt about it. My mother had turned my father into a mere empty calabash using witchcraft.

This is not to say that other wives in the village did not have some sort of influence on their husbands. They did. Except that they were more discreet and more diplomatic. In public, they would, as tradition requires, let their husbands prevail as masters of their households. The lion had to be kept roaring for the sake of appearance. In the privacy of the bedroom, however, women were said to be the real masters of the household. It is in the secrecy of the conjugal room and bed that the real decisions were made, and such decisions, the rumour went, were decisions imposed upon the village by women. Women ran the village, but gave the men the false honour of carrying the empty title of leaders of their households in public. The secret of these women's control was in their devilish use of their beauty, smile, nightly blackmail and witchcraft to control their husbands. This they would do without anyone noticing. A man once thought to be untamable would suddenly, after taking a new wife, become as docile as a baby lion. His voice would be heard booming less and less from his conjugal hut, and before long, the only voice being heard would be that of his wife. But most wives would take over their husbands with more diplomacy. If there were

33

some *medzo* in the village, they would let their men do the talking. If some event or gathering needed the presence of a member of the household, they would send their husbands. That's the way our customs wanted it to be. Women had the power of the inside and men the power of the outside.

But Mema was just no such diplomatic woman. She would attend every *medzo* in person. She would accompany her husband at every gathering and miss no opportunity to open her mouth. Even in the mud-walled church that the white man had come to build in our village in order to save our souls from the demon, my mother would impose her presence. For instance, when she found the preaching boring and not accurate enough according to what she knew of the Bible, she would interrupt the village catechist and take over the sermon. This would happen frequently during the daily morning prayers and even on Sundays when the whole village and people from neighbouring villages would gather for the big mass. The catechist lived my mother's interruptions as a trauma. He even came to see my mother as a messenger of the white man's devil, sent to this village in the form of a woman to test his faith. He had therefore resolved never to quit. He wanted to show the white man's God that he was indeed a true Christian, a true believer who would never give in when faced with such an obvious manifestation of the devil's presence on earth.

When a Sunday passed without my mother taking over the church to preach to the parishioners, the catechist would consider this a major victory against the forces of hell. He would be in very high spirits after the mass. He would greet everybody, and smile and laugh loudly, showing his happiness in whatever way he could. He would secretly bless our gods and publicly render grace to the white man's God, thanking them all for making him lucky and protecting him against the humiliation that loomed over him whenever Mema was in attendance. And since Mema never missed a mass or a daily prayer, the catechist was thought to be living his small hell on earth already.

But he was not lucky all the time. Whenever my mother took over the preaching slot of the service, she would really take over. She would spring up from her seat like a bow and turn around to face the audience. From there, she would with surprising expertise hammer the word of God with more power than the catechist could ever hope to achieve. The catechist, sweating from the rainy season's heat that was steaming into the church from the outside, would stand there, expressionless and humiliated. Then, after a while, he would simply walk back to his seat. There, heavily pained and unable to look into the eyes of his parishioners, he would put his head into his sorry hands and weep silently. Meanwhile, my mother would continue to hammer the Word with power, illustrating her preaching with live examples taken directly from the daily experiences of our people. Without mentioning specific names, she would allude to a well-known infidelity and ask why the culprits dared to come to church when they knew they were sinning so shamelessly. Did they not know the commandment of God that said that one should not go to bed with someone else's wife or husband? And so she went on and on, pointing fingers at the sins of these and at the lies of those, without citing specific names. And when she mentioned the horrible punishments that awaited the sinners in hell after they presented themselves at the locked gates of heaven, a chill of fear would be felt in the church that would freeze the blood of the parishioners in their veins. My mother's mouth would talk, talk and talk. When her mouth finally stopped spitting all the horrors of the white man's hell she could think of, a long bewildered silence would follow. After which the parishioners would be looking forward to a prompt end to the service so that they could rush home to drown their anguish in the numbing alcohol of their *malamba* brew.

But that was not all. Mema's fits of anger were also notorious in our village. When my mother was angry, the earth itself would stop breathing. When provoked or offended, Mema would boil herself into fits of rage that would shake the village from top to bottom like a volcanic explosion of lava. She would roar like a lioness whose newly born cubs had been devoured by a flock of famished hyenas. At moments such as those, she was not to be approached.

Because undiplomatic wives were so noticeable in my village as well as in many other villages in our area, my mother was feared by most women and dreaded by most men. And since her mouth possessed both the arrogance of the youth, and the wisdom and wit of the most prominent wisemen and wisewomen of our area, she had managed to build a solid reputation as one of the most skilful, although hated, speakers of our village. And she made it her duty to attend the most serious cases that were publicly tried in the *aba* hut situated in the centre of the village. It is in the *aba* that public *medzo* were tried by the community, and my mother would never leave a session of *medzo* without having spoken her mind in one way or another.

Unconventional behaviour such as my mother's had to be explained. Such behaviour was just not normal. There had to be more to it than that. As could be expected, she was accused by ill-intentioned mouths of being an *nnem* whose *évouss* and witchcraft were so powerful that she had managed to subdue not only her own husband, but also all the prominent people, males and females, of my village. Because part of our customs admired strong women, Mema was therefore both admired and loathed, respected and feared. Of course, my mother did just what could be expected from her: she took a devilish pleasure in fortifying her reputation and sowing awe amongst our people.

My father, I heard, left our world because of an unspecified disease. He lost his fight against a disease whose name cannot be translated into the white man's language, probably because the white man did not yet know the kind of diseases people used to die from in my village. Did my mother tell me the name of this disease? Perhaps. If she did, I have long since forgotten. I regret not being able to remember the name of the disease my father died from.

My father had spent most of his last years going from one *nguegan* to another. The sufferings of my mother began when she started to spend most of her time taking her husband to the various medicine men and women of our area. She had elected to try all sorts of medicines. But neither the witchdoctors nor their medicines cured my father. After several years of agony taking her husband to all known witchdoctors, Mema decided, out of desperation, to take her husband to a renowned *mimbiri* doctor in the village of Kom. She immediately encountered violent opposition from her husband's family, who despised and feared the *mimbiri* witchcraft and doctors. They argued that the fearful witchcraft known as *mimbiri* had come from foreign lands, from people against whom the Fang had fought fierce battles in the past. As a consequence, it was not trustworthy. Besides, they argued, it had resulted in more deaths than cures.

My mother did not yield.

She took her husband to the *mimbiri* doctor.

The *mimbiri* ceremonies required some weeks of preparation

before the trip to the world of the dead could be undertaken by the patient. This gave my mother's in-laws time to send delegation after delegation, speaker after speaker, to try to talk my mother out of risking the life of her husband in the dangerous ceremonies of *mimbiri*.

To no avail.

My mother turned a deaf ear to all warnings and threats, and persisted in her belief that the *mimbiri* witchcraft was her last chance to save her man.

'My husband,' she would declare to those who came to see her, 'will eat the bitter root and travel to his ancestors to beg for a cure. I have suffered too much taking him all over the place in search of a cure. Nothing has worked. So I say: this is our last chance. If there is a god out there, and if there are ancestors out there that are still caring for us, then let them cure my husband this time. My husband will travel to his dead people.'

'But, woman, haven't you, yourself, heard the white priest say that the *mimbiri* is evil medicine, and that because it is evil medicine, he will exclude from his church all the people who go and seek a cure from *mimbiri* doctors? Have you not heard him say that to become a disciple of *mimbiri* is to become a disciple of the devil? Are you ready to risk exclusion from the world of God because of your stubborn head?'

'Well, if that is so, then tell your white priest to go and eat the *mebi* of his own goats. What has his God done for my husband? I have prayed to his white God ever since my husband became ill. Now look at him. His health has grown worse day after day. I have even taken him to the country of Camelon where white priests are said to heal people with holy water. They did not manage to heal my husband. Even the white medicine that is practised in the town of Oyem here in our own land failed. The white doctors there told me that they could not tell what my husband was suffering from. They dismissed us from the hospital because they needed the beds for people they could cure. So I am asking you: what has their white God done for me? And what has the white man done for me? Nothing! Let the white priest excommunicate me. But I know that if there is a god in the clouds, he has seen my suffering and he will understand me. My husband will travel to his dead people to ask for a cure. That is what I have decided and nobody will make me change my mind!'

And so persisted the stubborn woman. One day before my father's journey to the village of the dead, the angered in-laws of my mother appeared on the path that led to the *mimbiri* camp. Obviously, they had come for the final battle. The daughters of my father's village, who according to our customs considered themselves the sisters of my father, were led by Akoure Okang, my father's elder sister. Akoure was the fiercest hater of my mother. The two women had never been able to get along very well because they had the same stubborn and rebellious temperament. When both women were in the village at the same time, peace was always broken by their constant wrangling. My mother, and above all the rest of the villagers, found peace only when Akoure went away to marry a man from the village of Ebang. But each of her visits was always dreaded because people knew that confrontation with my mother was inevitable.

So, when Akoure heard that my mother had taken her brother to the *mimbiri*, she went crazy. She not only rallied to her crusade those among her own sisters who had been married away, but also came back to our village, which was her native village, to rally her other village sisters. A group of thirty women went to war against my mother. And here they were, marching towards the camp like an army of invaders, ready to strike. People knew these women had come for battle because they all wore pieces of cloth tightly secured around their waists. The bottoms of their dresses were also tightly secured to prevent accidental viewing of what was underneath. In my village, when women were so dressed, one could assume that they were ready for battle, ready to engage in physical wrestling to save their honour. Their faces were stern, deformed by the anger they had all been nurturing since my mother decided to take their brother to the *mimbiri* medicine man.

My mother was sitting near the bamboo bed on which her husband was resting. The agonized man had been brought outside under the shade of the banana trees to get some fresh air and be given some medicinal herbs. His look was hazy and his eyes seemed to be fixed on an invisible object that nobody else could see. He appeared absent and did not give the impression of being able to hear all the noise that was starting to build up. He seemed totally unconscious of his surroundings. When my mother saw the group of people coming down the path that led to the *mimbiri* doctor's camp, she immediately knew who they were. She did not budge from her seat. She just looked down, seized by some sort of unusual sadness, and waited. The people in the camp slowly gathered around this arriving group, out of curiosity. They knew that war was underway.

'Ah Ntsame Minlame, stubborn woman,' roared Akoure Okang, my father's elder sister. 'We have come to get Sima Okang from you to take him home. We will not let the sorceress that you are kill him by offering his soul to the *bezaran*, the devils, of those *mimbiri* people. Today, Sima Okang, my younger brother, will go back to the village of our father with us. Today, whether you want it or not, he will return with us. You have played too much with us already. Today we are going to show you who we really are. Do you think that a little woman like you is going to order everyone around as you have been doing? No! We are going to kill your arrogance. Do you hear me?'

My mother remained seated and silent, as if not listening. Her gaze was directed at her suffering husband.

'Ah Ntsame, I am speaking to you. Has your tongue been cut? I said I have come to get back my brother and take him away from your evil. Do you hear me?'

Silence. Same absent gaze from my mother.

'I am repeating, impolite woman, that I have come to get my brother, and I will not leave today without him. I am Akoure Okang, daughter of Okang Nnang, the same man whose *knon* gave life to the man you are trying to kill. If it is true that I was the first child who came out of my mother's belly, then I speak here today with the tongue of my dead mother and father. If it is true that it is my eyes that first saw the light of the day, then I speak here today as both the father and mother of my family. If it is true that it is my mouth that first drank the blood of my mother's *ébón* when my head came out of her belly, then today I am also speaking as the mother of your husband. And I say: I will not leave today without him.'

My aunt's face was contorting into a frightening rage that left the crowd's insides compressed, as if from a lack of air. Her nostrils were dilated and she was breathing heavily as she spoke. Her words hammered the air, hitting as hard as the sticks of a drummer trying to get from his huge tom-tom all the sounds that it could produce. Her words were like the fierce roar of the drums lifting and shaking the hearts and bowels inside the dancers' chests, guiding their movements and causing an uncontrollable frenzy of feet, hands, hips and heads. Akoure, my aunt, was not a woman to play with. She had the reputation of being the tigress of her family. She was a she-bull always ready to attack. When she was in this state of anger, she was as stubborn

41

as a rock. That is why she did not listen to the elders of the village when they tried to convince her of the futility of her decision. They thought the situation required diplomacy, above all because at the end of it stood Ntsame Minlame, the woman who had become the terror of all in the village and beyond. Did her name, which meant 'destroyer of villages', not tell it all? Ntsame Minlame had come to our village to destroy it. Let's not allow her to do so by responding to her provocations. Diplomacy in dealing with her is always better than a frontal attack. But Akoure was no diplomat. She liked to look her enemies straight in the eyes, and was always ready to pounce on them like a starving panther.

The crowd was now silent, as if suddenly hit by an unexpected bolt of lightning that crippled them, freezing them into lifeless statues on the spot.

'Hear me well, woman,' Akoure continued to thunder. 'Hear me well because your impolite silence will not help you today. If my brother stays a day longer in this abominable place of witchcraft, then you can take my name away from me.'

As she spoke these words, Akoure turned to her following and shouted out the name of a young male.

'Ekang Mba!'

'*Owé, ah nnah* Akoure.'

'If it is true that I am your aunt and that the man lying there is my brother, if it is true that I am the elder of all sons and daughters of our whole family, from the belly of my mother's sister to the belly of my father's brother, then I say it is time to go. I say, help your uncle to his feet and put him on the *tipoi* we brought for him. We will carry him home at once.'

'*Owé, ah nnah* Akoure. I hear you well. Mbira! Help me put my uncle on the *tipoi* so we can carry him home.'

Upon hearing these words, my mother suddenly awoke from

42

her dazed torpor. She sprang to her feet like an arrow from a bow.

'*Song!*' she thundered, pointing a threatening finger at the feet of Ekang Mba and Mbira Ndong, who had not even had time to move a foot. '*Song!*' she said, sending a chill into the crowd as she hammered the scary word of death with all the vigour in her voice. '*Song*' was one of the scariest words in our language. It literally meant 'cemetery', a word which, when directed at someone in particular, we understood as meaning 'Move a finger and you will find yourself dead at the cemetery.' The word froze people on the spot, like a curse.

'*Song!*' my mother repeated. 'I say "*song!*" to both of you and to all others who would want to lose their heads today.'

A sharpened and shiny machete had suddenly appeared in the hands of my mother. She lifted the weapon in the air, ready to strike. The crowd scattered in panic. Some shut themselves up in their *mendah*, firmly securing their doors. Others hid behind the nearby banana trees, ready to throw themselves into the forest should the mad woman come any closer.

Akoure's people had taken immediate flight, hiding even farther away from this woman whose craziness they knew from long ago. They knew that when she said she was going to cut a throat, she really meant it. Nothing would stop her. They remembered an episode from a few years back when she almost killed her own husband, this very man that she was now desperately trying to heal. My mother, they remembered, had had a quarrel with her husband. The quarrel had begun in the hut, but my mother had made it public by deciding to come and shout at her husband from outside the hut. Because of this, the dispute ended up being witnessed by the rest of the village. As usual, it was Ntsame Minlame doing the talking, while her subdued husband listened. But Ntsame did not like to see things happening that way. She wanted a fight with her husband. She found it disgraceful to her and to manhood itself that he should always stay silent whenever they had an argument. She wanted him to react to her anger, to do or say something that would add dry wood to the bush fire burning inside her. Something that would keep the fire going and growing. Something that would turn tiny match flames into a wild, uncontrollable conflagration that would devour everything it encountered on its path, be it humans, trees, river waters, birds, insects or animals. She wished for the fire of devastation to descend onto the earth from the skies. She wished for a fire that would tell the world that the wrath of the gods was upon all and that there was no escape. She wanted all the beings of creation to know that the moment of reckoning had arrived and that no place of hiding would be safe now – that the fire of the gods would always know where to find them. Those hiding in caves would be suffocated, for there would be no clean air to breathe. Those hiding in tree trunks would be turned into charcoal and become nourishment to the starved and famished earth. Those hiding in water would be cooked alive and become food for the fishes. Those flying in the skies would be snatched from mid-air by the tongues of the angry flames, and dragged down into the underworld of eternal suffering.

Yes, her husband drove her crazy like a bush fire whenever he sat there in silence, listening with maddening indifference to the barkings that came from her mouth. She wished he were as angry as she was. She wished he would, at least once in a while, decide to fight back and take away from her shoulders the weight of the world that she was carrying. But her husband was of a soft, placid and subdued nature. He could let an elephant wrap its trunk around his neck and tear off his head without even trying to seek shelter or defend himself. It was precisely this subdued character of my father's that infuriated the woman to the point of madness.

'What kind of a man are you?' she would shout in those situations. 'What kind of man are you to stand there like a dead tree, and not speak to me? People! Look at him! I am speaking to him, but he stands there like a bull whose penis has been cut off, an impotent bull who can no longer perform on a female. Is that the kind of man that my parents gave me? A man who cannot even give me a child? All the young girls married to this village, including my own little sister, have all had children. Why not me? What did I do to the *beyem* of this village who have been eating my children in my belly so that I would not give birth? Shame, Sima Okang. I say shame to you!'

My father was a pacifist. But in those situations, in situations where his so-called impotence was publicly shouted out to the entire village, even a pacifist and lame man like him would attempt to defend his honour. That day, as if suddenly transfigured, he seized my mother by the neck and applied his anger to beating her up. Of course, she would fight back, that crazy woman, wrestling her husband to the ground and trying to lacerate his skin with both her nails and teeth. But her man had had enough.

'I am going to teach you who I am today,' said my unrecognizable father. 'I am going to teach you who is the master in this hut.'

These would be the only words my father would utter on those days when the spirits of anger descended upon him to possess his soul and lead him to crime. At these moments, he would not say much, but his hands would be doing the talking for him. To his hands, my mother's mouth would respond. She would first call the names of all the people in the village, begging them to rescue her. Then, she would change her mind and

45

demand that her husband kill her. 'Kill me! Kill me!' she would repeat, throwing herself at her husband for more punishment. 'Wooooohhh! He is killing me, people! Can you see, he is killing me!'

Of course, those times when the bull in my father finally awoke were so cherished by the villagers that no one would budge a finger to defend the arrogant woman. 'At last!' people would silently mutter with appreciation and relief. At last he was showing her who carried an *nkon* between his legs in that hut. Let no one intervene, they would say. Let him teach her a lesson. She looked for it.

But my mother was a very resourceful woman. Seeing that the villagers were not intervening to save her from the claws of her man, as they would normally do when other husbands beat their wives, she suddenly ran to her kitchen hut, and came out with a machete, seemingly ready to slash her husband into pieces. This time, the villagers thought, she was really crazy. The crowd of people that had come closer dispersed in panic. Seeing that this was no time to hang about, her husband ran for his life too, with my mother at his heels. 'Stop there if you are a man,' she would order. 'Stop there and show me your manhood now, impotent goatshit. Show me how you can beat me up with this machete in my hands.'

'Stop her! Stop the mad woman,' my father would shout, still running ahead of my mother so fast that he could have been mistaken for one of the younger runners of our village. Eventually, my mother would stop, exhausted and breathing heavily from chasing her husband throughout a village that had been suddenly deserted by people running for their lives.

'Sima Okang!' she called, still breathing heavily. 'I say to you: "*Song!*" If you do not stop running now, I will cut my throat and kill myself.'

My father stopped at a good distance, yelling words to her from afar.

'Now don't be stupid, woman. Stop playing the fool, calm down and go home to your hut.'

'You think I am playing?' she retorted. 'Then look . . .'

My mother lifted her machete very high above her head, and downed it directly onto her forearm, cutting a huge gash in the red flesh from which a stream of warm blood gushed. She fainted immediately, unable to withstand the horror of her erupting blood. A cry of disbelief rose up from the village: 'Elders and forefathers of the Essangwame clan! She has killed herself!' The panicked and horrified village people ran to rescue her, and took her to her hut to cure the wound. 'Where have you ever seen a crazy woman like Ntsame Minlame?' they asked one another, bewildered as they were by an event whose outcome they could never have anticipated. But then again, why should they be amazed? With Ntsame Minlame, you could always expect anything.

◆

And here she was going again. A lifted machete. A designated enemy. Her crazy spirits on her again. She was ready for the kill. Everybody knew. Everybody ran. Except Akoure Okang, who, in her panic, had tripped and fallen down like a basket of cassava. My mother was now towering over her, ready to finish her off with a single blow. She barked:

'Akoure Okang. I know you are my sister-in-law, the first child who came out of the *ébón* of my husband's mother. But I am asking you today: do you want to die? I am asking again: do you really want to die? Because if you want to die, say it and let me cut your throat now. I say I will cut your throat without

47

regret, but my husband will not move from here, do you hear me? I have had enough of you and your family beating me up and violating me with your vipers' tongues. I have had enough of your people treating me like goatshit. You have called me a sorceress, you have accused me of being a witch. I say to all of you today that if you do not leave this place at once, you are going to see the real witch in me. If you do not leave me in peace, blood is going to flow. Otherwise, you can take my name away from me.'

'Ntsame Minlame, crazy woman. Witch! You do not have any respect for anyone. Don't you know I am your husband? Now you want to eat my blood. You brought my brother here to kill him, and now you want to eat my blood too. But I will not leave. Kill me. I will die here with my brother, but I will not leave.'

'Akoure!' cried voices from the crowd. 'For the sake of our ancestors, leave. Do not be as stubborn as that crazy woman. Just leave and let the gods curse her for her insolence and lack of respect for our customs. We plead with you, ah Akoure! Please, let us leave and let the curse of our forefathers destroy her.' But Akoure was even more stubborn than my mother, a stubbornness that almost cost her her life that day. As promised, my mother did indeed lift her machete and bring it down mercilessly on her sister-in-law. Fortunately for Akoure Okang, Ekang Mba and Mbira Ndong were quicker than my mother's machete. They each grabbed an arm of the woman on the ground and pulled the reckless Akoure away from under a machete that would inevitably have sent her sulking to the world of the ancestors.

My mother did go ahead and let her husband take the trip to the world of the dead to ask for a cure. He ate the mixture of bitter roots, sacred leaves, human-bone powder and other secret ingredients concocted by the *mimbiri* priest that were to help him travel from the world of the living to the world of the dead. If things went as planned, he was expected to come back with a cure. But my father never came back. He died right there on his mystical trip mat.

What had happened? Nobody really knew. He died right there. The *mimbiri* doctor said that, while playing his *engombe*-zither and singing his incantation songs, he had himself travelled along with my father. He had seen to it that my father had travelled well, and indeed Pepa's mystical trip had begun well. He had greeted all his ancestors and had met his own deceased father and mother Okang Nnang and Akoma Mba. He had told them about his disease and informed them that he had come to the world of the dead to ask for health and healing. After listening to his long story of illness, the dead took mercy on him. They promised they would cure him, and that he just had to wait a few hours to allow them to discuss the best cure for him. The spirits of the dead asked him to wait in the *aba* at the centre of their village while they consulted. Sima Okang sat in the *aba*, happily enjoying the fact that he had been able to see his ancestors, and above all his dead parents. He now knew they were well, and was grateful to the gods of the clan, and to Zame ya Mebegue, the great great one himself. He now just had to wait for his cure, which he was confident the dead people would bring to him.

'But Sima,' said the *mimbiri* doctor, 'had made a fatal mistake during his trip. While waiting in the *aba*, he was joined by the spirit of his dead mother who brought him food. And since he was hungry from having eaten nothing for so many days, he ate the food his mother had brought with delight. Yet a respectable *mimbiri* doctor like I am always advises his patients never to accept the food given to them by the dead. Everybody here knows that I told Sima to refuse the food that I knew the *Bekon* would be giving him during his trip. It is well known to all that the *Bekon*, before giving you their cure, will constantly try you to see if you are a respectable person. Giving you food is one of the tests by which they can determine whether you are capable of abiding by the advice of the *mimbiri* doctor who sent you to them. When you eat the dead people's food, you fail the test because you have in fact chosen food over your cure. Unfortunately, according to the laws of the dead, you can never come back from their village alive after giving your life away in such a detestable manner. Sima disobeyed my advice.

'This is why,' the *mimbiri* doctor hammered, 'he died. I am telling you, had he not eaten that food, he would have come back and I would have been able to cure him with the sacred herbs whose names the *Bekon* people would have given him. Usually, people to whom the ghosts promise relief survive and are cured. People die only when they do not follow the instructions given to them by me or the *Bekon* themselves. The ones who die during the trip or after are those who ate the food or those whom the ghosts refused to cure because they thought their situation was now in the hands of Zame ya Mebegue himself. Why did Sima eat that food, mmmh? Tell me, why did he eat that food?'

But my mother's pains were not over. She was still mourning the death of her husband and getting ready to have the body carried back to the village when her two daughters also fell mysteriously ill. They were my little sisters. One was only one *mbuh* younger than me, and the other was two *mimbuh* away from me. So, on the day following the death of my father, they both inexplicably died.

This was a terrible blow to my mother.

Mema.

Mother.

My mother.

My mother had a hard time in life conceiving her first child. Her childless situation was so desperate that people in the village started to believe that my father had married himself a barren woman. Her situation was made worse by the fact that her little sister, Mema Afome, had been able to give birth to four children out of the nine that she eventually had, before my mother could conceive her first son. What was more, Mema Afome had married into the same village to a cousin of the clan of my father. The presence of her very fertile younger sister was a constant reminder to Mema of her infertile state. She had learned to live with the idea that she might be totally barren and unable to give birth to a child. In the meantime she consoled herself with the children of her sister who, according to our customs, were also hers. She undertook to raise all of the first four children of her younger sister as if they were her own, taking them under her custody as soon as they were able to do without the breast milk of their mother. Of course, because her sister was able to lay children as quickly as a hen would eggs, my mother was getting even more uncomfortable. She did not feel any kind of jealousy towards her sister, but the fact that Mema Afome was able to have children almost at will made my mother's situation even more desperate in a society where children were the best thing that could happen to a woman. Children were a promise of grandness, for by becoming a mother a woman entered the realm of motherhood and reaped the fruits of the social respect that was attached to the status of mother. Mema, the elder daughter of her mother's belly, reaped those fruits only much later than her younger sister.

Of course, my mother attributed her bad luck to the bad eye. There were certainly some *beyem* in the village who hated her and who must have been eating her children in her belly before they were conceived. People had even started to suggest to her husband that he should take a second wife in order to make sure that he had heirs who would multiply the family blood after him. But my mother would not have it. She would stand outside her kitchen hut and hammer publicly into the heads of her husband and his people that another woman would never cross the threshold of her hut, and that the day her husband decided to bring one home, she would be waiting for them with her machete. And thus she would bark outside for a while, accusing everybody of bad intentions towards her and ordering them to stop their witchcraft. If they did not stop, she threatened, she would go and consult a powerful witchdoctor who would reveal the names of those who had been eating her children in her belly.

The threats seem to have worked because, eventually, my mother did get pregnant with my elder brother. At last! It was a miracle. At first she did not believe it. She did not want to believe it. She did not want to tell the good news to anyone before she was sure. Not even to her husband. Also, she did not want to disappoint herself. She had awaited this moment for so long that if she came to believe in the possibility, and the possibility ended up a fallacy, she did not know if she could survive such a blow. So she remained unconvinced. Or, at least, she tried to remain unconvinced. Her doubts were strong. But at times her doubts were mixed with hopes. And her hopes kept her sleepless at night. Every morning, she would wake up and go behind the hut to look for signs of her monthly indication of barrenness. She would see no blood. Reassured, she would continue to hope. She would be hoping and doubting, but also doubting and hoping.

So, for the first three months, Mema was very careful with her belly. She reduced her working hours and avoided carrying heavy loads. At night, she refused her husband's solicitations for fear that his pounding her insides with his *nkon* would cause some tearing that would totally compromise her chances.

After the first three months, all her doubts evaporated. She was at last convinced that this was it. She got confirmation of this when other women in the village started to make remarks about her skin colour, which had gone from a shiny dark to a shiny brown, her growing belly and her malaises. She took those comments with the pride of a woman who knew she was going to become a mother. When she finally told this to her husband, he could not believe it. To help her protect the pregnancy, he decided that from now on, he would be both the man and the woman of the house. He would cook, wash, plant, fetch water and attend to all her needs. Happiness had finally come their way and they were going to make sure it stayed. A new surge of love and caring seized my parents, and together they prayed to the gods of our clan, asking them to safely bring the baby to life and protect it against the evil of the *beyem*.

So, when she realized the pregnancy was real and that the baby seemed to have come to stay, my mother chose to travel to the land of Camelon to give birth at Akom. Akom was the village of her maternal uncles, that is to say, the village of her mother. There, she thought, she would be able to protect her baby from the bad eye that had been eating her belly in Otongwaku, the village of her husband.

But my mother was wrong.

In Akom, she was witness to one of the strangest happenings of her life. She had just recently, the gods be thanked, given birth to my elder brother and was living in a kitchen-hut that had been allocated to her. My mother had taken with her one of my cousins, the third child of my aunt. This child loved Mema more than he did his own mother. How could he not? Like most of the children of my aunt, he had been raised by Mema since he was taken off his mother's breast. Elouma Ze had therefore always preferred to live with my mother. When my mother decided to travel to Camelon to give birth away from the evil of Otongwaku, Elouma Ze made it clear Mema would not leave without taking him with her. For days, he sulked. Then, on the day of my mother's departure, Elouma threw himself to the ground and cried and kicked and threatened to hurt himself if he was not allowed to go with my mother. It was thus decided that he should go with her. Besides, people argued, it was always good to have a child around who could run some errands. My mother would later thank the ancestors for Elouma's presence.

Here is how the incredible story went.

One morning, my mother felt like going to the bushes behind her maternity hut to relieve herself from a stomach discomfort that had been haunting her for a few days. The family shithole used for that effect was not too far away. A crying baby could easily be heard from there. She felt at peace with her short absence because she had left Elouma with the charge of watching over the newly born baby. At that time, Elouma must have been only about five *mimbuh*. My mother was already squatting over the family shithole when she heard the small voice of Elouma calling out from the kitchen-hut.

'Mema! Mema! Mema!' the boy shouted. 'An old woman is trying to take the baby! Don't touch my mother's baby, you old woman. Do not touch him! Go away! Go away! Go away!'

Alarmed, my mother came rushing back to the hut, struggling to tie her cloth around her waist as she ran.

'What's going on in here?' she asked, entering the hut like a raging hurricane. 'Oh, it is you, Mema Akouma? What's going on?'

'Mema, Mema,' the boy said. 'Look! She wanted to take the baby. That old woman is bad. She wanted to take the baby, but I defended the baby. Don't let her take my little brother. That woman is bad. Really bad.'

'What a strange child,' old Akouma observed. 'I just wanted to see your baby. I heard some days ago that you had given birth to a boy child. Since I have not yet had the time to come and see him, I just wanted to pay a visit to give you my greetings and hold him a little bit. Oh what a beautiful little boy you have here, ah Ntsame. What a beautiful little boy. Can I hold him?'

'No!' intervened little Elouma Ze again, defiantly standing in front of the bamboo cradle in which Owono Sima, my mother's first child, was sleeping. 'No, Mema Ntsame! Do not let her touch my little brother. Do not let her. She is bad. She is a bad woman!'

Puzzled, my mother had to give in to Elouma's request, jokingly brushing it aside as the misbehaviour of a child who felt protective of his mother's baby and did not want to let strangers touch him.

'Well, *ah nnah* Akouma. You see, my little husband here has decided that no one should touch the baby. Besides, as you can see, the baby is still sleeping and I do not want him to wake up now. But do not worry, I am still here for a few months, so I am sure you will get to hold him before my return to Ngabon.'

'*Owé*, I hear you, *ah* Ntsame. I will come back later. And you, little boy, why are you being nasty to your grandmother? You see, I just wanted to see the baby. Are you jealous that I would marry the baby, and not you? Ooohhhh! Yes, I see, that's it. You are jealous.'

'No, you are lying,' said little Elouma Ze, wilder than ever. 'I know you are lying. You wanted to take my mother's baby away.'

'Come on now, Elouma, leave old Mema Akouma alone. Don't you see she is a nice, beautiful woman? Don't you want to marry her?'

'Me? Marry her? Nooooohhh!! She . . . she is too old, and I . . . I . . . I am still too little. Besides, she is not beautiful, and she is bad.'

'I will cook you good food, my little husband,' said *nnah* Akouma as she left the hut. 'Then I am sure you will love me, little husband. Peace to you and your family, *ah* Ntsame.'

'Peace to you also, *ah nnah* Akouma.'

My mother remained silent for a while, wondering what all this meant. Why was old Akouma coming to her maternity hut so early? And why did little Elouma Ze react so violently against her? Ah, these children. So my mother dismissed the whole event and went back to the rear of the hut to finish her relief effort at the family shithole. She did not have the time to undo her waist cloth before little Elouma Ze started to shout out to her again: 'Mema! Mema! Mema! The old lady is back again! She wants to take the baby.'

My mother, again, ran back to the hut. She found old Akouma standing in front of little Elouma, who was fiercely protecting the cradle.

'*Ah nnah* Akouma, it's you again? What is wrong now?' my mother asked.

'Well, I have just come back to see the baby again. But this little boy is really being bad today.'

'But I thought I told you to come back later to see the baby?'

'Yes, but I just thought I could see him now. Why don't you wake him up so I can hold him?'

'No, Mema Akouma. That baby kept me awake all night

57

long. I need some rest. I would like him to sleep well so that I can get some rest too. Come back later.'

The old lady left, although reluctantly. My mother was speechless. What strange behaviour!

About two cock crows later, cries broke out from all over the village. Someone had just died. The deceased person was old Akouma. 'Old Akouma!?' my mother exclaimed. 'This was the old woman who just this morning came to my hut to see the baby. How is that possible?'

My mother was told that old *nnah* Akouma had just been found dead in her hut by her drunken husband. Her body was still warm. What killed her? No one really knew. But, when my mother told the village about what had happened earlier in the day, those with the knowledge understood.

In my land, those who knew things explained that there were two sorts of people. On the one hand, there were the *mimimyè*. On the other, there were the *beyem*.

The *mimimyè* were the innocent, those with innocent souls who literally knew nothing. They were like children in a world of adults and did not have an *évouss* strong enough to see beyond the visible world. Therefore, anyone who was an *nmimyè* was at the constant mercy of the evil of the *beyem*.

The *beyem* were those villagers who knew; they were the knowers, the omniscients. They knew everything about the world of the visible, but also about the frightening, mystical world of the invisible. They knew everything about the *mimimyè* villagers and could do what they wanted with their souls.

The *beyem* themselves were divided into two groups. There were the good *beyem*, those who did not want to use their mystical might to harm others. Because they were good, their job was to protect the *mimimyè* against the evil *beyem*. The good *beyem*, when they had an exceptionally stronger power than the average *beyem*, often became *minguegan*, and thus acted as a mystical counterweight to the evil *beyem*. The *minguegan* would thus act as diviners, medicine men and witchdoctors, and as such, were able to undo the evil deeds of the bad *beyem*.

The evil *beyem* were feared in all the villages of my land. They made use of their evil powers to eat other villagers. At night, their spirits would leave their bodies and travel around the world performing all sorts of evil acts and eating people. They would fight amongst themselves for the control of the spirits of the *mimimyè* people and they would arrange the order in which they would eat the innocent villagers. At night, when the night owls began their lugubrious concerts, it was never advised to go out. One had to stay in and pray that nobody in the family would be the target of tonight's evil feasting. Nightly owl gatherings were always the frightening sign of an ongoing feasting and villagers knew that they could expect a suspect death in the village in the next few days. Sometimes, the *beyem* would disguise their crimes. Instead of eating the whole spirit of their victim, which would cause real death in the real world, they would eat only an arm. And this, in the day following the feasting, would translate into someone inexplicably losing an arm in a strange accident. The *mimimyè* villagers therefore lived in constant fear of being eaten by the *beyem*, above all by jealous *beyem* who would envy the success of one's son in life, or the wealth of one's household.

It was not easy to know who among the villagers was an evil *nnem*. Someone could be married to a wife or a husband who was an *nnem* and not know it. Worse, an *nnem*'s body could be sleeping heavily by your side and you would not know that the owner of that body was actually away eating people. When the *beyem* travelled at night, they left their bodies behind in order not to betray themselves. To travel, they borrowed the bodies of night owls, bodies that they used as mystical planes to travel to any part of the world in one single night and come back before dawn. Indeed, it was dangerous for the *beyem* who had gone out at night to be out until daytime. This would mean certain death for them.

Only good *beyem* were able to reveal to the villagers who among them was an *nnem*. But it was not easy for the good *beyem* to do so. They often had to fight hard to survive the mortal assaults of the evil ones, who wanted to get rid of any *nnem* who was likely to bring their nightly activities into public knowledge. At night, bad *beyem* would feast over the invisible body of the good *beyem*, and the latter would die in real life a few days or months later, according to how the *beyem* planned it.

In Akom, it came to be known that old Akouma was an *nnem* of the evil kind. That is why she died so suddenly. The evil *beyem*, the story went, had one huge weakness. Each time they went out at night to do evil, they would lose a lot of energy and would end up overusing their *évouss*. When this *évouss* could no longer allow them to travel at night to perform evil, they would fall mortally ill. Old Akouma, it was concluded, was in urgent need of a new *évouss*, having overused her own with constant nightly travels. A tired *évouss* meant an accelerated and certain death unless the *nnem* could quickly replace it with a new one. By going to my mother's hut, old Akouma was hoping that she would be able to swap her exhausted *évouss* with the new *évouss* of my mother's baby. All she needed in order to operate the transfer was to hold the baby in her arms. During that brief period of time, she would exhale her old *évouss* into the baby and inhale into herself the baby's brand-new *évouss*. That way she would prolong her lifespan, while the baby would suffer an inexplicable sudden death. But Elouma Ze, that awful little boy, had made it impossible for her to come close to the baby. He had saved my mother's first baby. Our ancestors be blessed for that.

Mema.

Mother.

My mother.

And here she was, my mother, at this *mimbiri* camp, with three dead bodies: her husband, whom she had come to cure, and the only two daughters that she had had after giving birth to my elder brother and myself. How could life be so cruel to her, a woman who had suffered so much? How could the gods do this to her? How could they pretend to heed her prayers by giving her a husband and four children, just to take half of her family away? What was the cruel punishment for? What were her sins? What was she accused of? Could anyone accuse her of having failed to pray and make offerings to the gods?

Prayers.

Before having her first child, she had said prayers in the night as well as in the day. She had said them in the forest as she walked to her farming fields, as she bathed in the forest stream and as she covered her body with special creams made out of sacred leaves that were destined to render her fertile like the earth after the rainy season. She had prayed for protection, for fertility, for health for her family, for life.

Indeed, her prayers had been heard in a wonderful way. She had ended up with the best combination of children any proud woman could hope for: two handsome boys and two beautiful girls. Her dream was that when the girls were of an age to be married, she would be able to use their brideprices to marry wives to her two sons. This would mean that each of her daughters, by getting married, was at the same time offering a wife to the brother with whom she was paired. My mother was happy that the gods had given her such a wonderful combination of children. What a blessing!

Now all those dreams, all those blessings were being shattered by the abomination that had befallen her at this *mimbiri* camp. How was this possible? Why had the ancestors decided to take away with one hand what they had given her with another? She had feared, had even known, that she would lose her sickly husband one day. That, she could accept because it had always been a matter of time. He was too ill and all her efforts to find a cure for him had proved unsuccessful. But why did the gods hide from her that she was also going to lose her two girl children at the same time? Who has ever mourned and buried both father and children on the same day? Was this the work of the gods or the work of the evil of men?

Prayers. Ancestors. Prayers. Gods. Prayers.

She had prayed for relief, not for pain. She had seen witchdoctor after witchdoctor, and travelled long distances for her husband.

Her husband.

An exceptional man who, for all their problems, had nevertheless been the best man she could have found. When they met for the first time he was young and strong, yet so calm and self-effacing. She loved him enormously. Their marriage had been a good marriage. Her fights with him had just been her own capricious way of making sure the relationship was one of love, not of formality. And he loved her too, for despite all that his parents said about her, he always stood by her, supporting her all along. And now, her man, her *ayem* tree, her protector, her unfaltering supporter, was leaving her. And he was taking away half of their family with him. Was this in punishment? But then, what had she done that was wrong? Could the ancestors punish her for trying to cure her husband? Or was it rather that all the *beyem* of the world of the humans had leagued themselves against her? But for what purpose? Had she not been just a woman in search of what was good for her husband and children? Like everyone else, she knew that all living beings in the village of the humans as well as in that of the animals were doomed to join the land of the ancestors. Joining the ancestors was never a problem for anyone, as long as things happened the proper and right way.

The right way. The proper way.

People would know for certain, when things happened the right way. They could tell when death occurred properly. This death, these deaths did not occur properly. They hid something terrible within themselves, a gloomy sign, a lugubrious message that meant something. Nothing in this universe happened at random. There was always a cause, and there was always an explanation. But how would she be able to explain such an occurrence? Three persons who were under her care had just died in the space of two days, for no apparent reason. This was certainly not common. This was an abomination. A crime. But who committed it?

My mother blamed the family of her husband for the crimes, above all Akoure Okang. They had, she claimed, eaten her two daughters in order to avenge themselves. They had even gone so far as to eat their own son and brother so that the world could put the blame on her.

Of course, my father's family blamed my mother for the crimes. It was not as she said, they argued. They had nothing to do with it. Had they not warned their brother that this woman was full of witchcraft? Had the white priest not warned all the Christians in our area against going to those *mimbiri* devils? Had the white priest not threatened to throw Ntsame Minlame

63

out of the church of his God in order to punish her for consulting the *mimbiri* doctors? Had he not said that the angry hand of his God would fall upon all those who dared to disobey, distributing punishments that would permit no deliverance? Was she not warned? Did she not know that those *mimbiri* doctors were evil *beyem* whose only purpose was to eat their patients? There was no doubt. She had willingly betrayed the whole family to the *mimbiri* spirits. She had eaten her husband and had not hesitated to eat her own daughters. And now she is blaming us? Pwah! Didn't we say?

Vanquished by the circumstances of her life, my mother did not have much more to say. She fell in a mute silence and never opened her mouth again. The pain had reached the boiling point in her heart and it felt as though her head was going to be shattered into thousands of small pieces. Life itself had become meaningless. She was ready to die. She wanted to rejoin her husband and daughters in the invisible world of the dead. She was sure she would feel no pain in the world of the ancestors. She no longer had the strength to fight.

Secret meetings were held by my father's people to decide the lot of my mother. Since she was a married woman, they could not force her to leave and go back to her family. Whether they wanted it or not, she was now part of the village. Furthermore, she had given the village new blood, although two of the children had now joined the ancestors in the company of their father. But it was the sacred duty of the village to protect the remaining children. These had to be taken away from her before she could have the opportunity to harm them too. The events in the life of that woman had shown that she could not be trusted. In fact, what had happened showed that she herself was an *nnem*, as they had always suspected. Nothing therefore guaranteed that she would not harm the remaining children. Nothing ensured that she would not betray them to the *mimbiri* doctors just as she had betrayed her husband and daughters. 'So,' said one of the village elders, 'the question we must ask ourselves is the following: would it be good for us to trust her with the blood of our village that flows in the veins of the remaining children, or would it be more prudent to take the children away and raise them ourselves? My position is that we should take the children and let her decide what she wants to do with herself. Do we agree?'

'*Owé!* We agree fully. Let us take the children from her,' the villagers concluded.

Several months passed, during which burial and mourning ceremonies and rites were performed. Sacrifices and prayers were offered to the gods and the spirits so that they could cleanse the village of the evil that had taken both father and daughters. An abomination like this one had never before been seen in our village. This probably meant that there was now too much evil in it. It could also mean that something had brought terrible bad luck to our people. The village therefore had to cleanse itself. For most people mourning and cleansing ceremonies were to last until three months after the burial. However, my mother, because she was both the widow of the deceased man and the mother of the two deceased children, had to continue to mourn for at least two years.

The village people, for reasons of decency, and above all because they wanted to allow the spirits of the dead to travel in peace, did not bring up the issue of the remaining children before the first year after the deaths of my father and sisters. They had kept their decision to take the remaining children away from my mother secret until then. Now, they felt the time had come to carry out their plans.

As had been decided during the secret meeting a year earlier, a party of elders and others set off to my mother's hut to claim the remaining children, now aged four and six *mimbuh* respectively. They forebade Akoure Okang, the most ferocious hater of my mother, to attend the *medzo* because they thought she would spoil the whole thing. Because my mother had been totally subdued for the past year, they thought they had a good chance of making her listen to the voice of reason.

They entered my mother's hut.

My mother remained silent.

They sat down.

My mother remained silent.

They spoke.

My mother listened.

They said they had come to get the children.

My mother asked them to say it again.

They said it again.

My mother showed them the machete.

They fled in panic.

She kept the children.

In the months that followed, they cursed her wherever they went, and missed no occasion to tell everyone of her devilishness.

In the months that followed, my mother remained silent.

Her husband's people did not speak to her for the next two *mimbuh*. My mother spoke to none of her husband's people for the next two *mimbuh*.

But she kept her children.

The village of the humans was a normal village, just like any human village. It had an *aba*, thatch-roofed huts from which rose the smoke from early morning fires. It had, standing behind its huts, banana, *sia*, papaya and avocado trees whose branches loomed like long arms over the roofs. It had poultry running wild in pursuit of flying insects, pigs and sheep running away from barking dogs. It had its own *gendarme* birds exercising their voices to the tune of the new day, and building nests in the branches of the plantain trees. A cold misty morning fog was covering everything. Its dewy fingers appeared to be loosening their invisible grip on the neck of the village, vanishing gradually and receding into the dark depths of the surrounding forest.

This village was a normal village.

Like many other normal villages, it was a smoky clearing in the jungle, mysterious, alive, awakening to the new day. A new day. A new life cycle. Birth followed by death. Death followed by birth. Over and over again. Day after day.

Human voices could now be heard. Echoing the morning voices were the dry coughs of old people whose overused bones had started to give way underneath them, bones no longer able to resist the process of ageing. To this morning music of awakening husky voices, pounding sticks held by women responded with surprising frenzy, offering their heavy rhythmic accompaniment to the unorchestrated cacophony of the dawn.

This was the village of Zame ya Mebegue. Zame ya Mebegue

was the patriarch of the village. He was the oldest man in the village, and the village was known by his name.

Zame ya Mebegue.

The village had once had a different name, but that name had long since been forgotten because of the deeds of Zame ya Mebegue. Did Zame ya Mebegue not wrestle a ghost in the forest for two years, and eventually win the fight? Did he not, in another exploit, escape death and save the village when he killed seven wild buffaloes with only one stone, and seven flies with only one strike? Zame ya Mebegue's deeds in this village had been so extraordinary that, from one end of the earth to the other, from the white man's land to the black man's land, from the world of the living to the world of the dead, this village came to be known as the village of Zame ya Mebegue.

But two *mimbuh* ago Zame ya Mebegue himself, who was now an old man, suddenly became ill. When one passed by his hut, one could hear the sound of sorrow mounting. Nothing seemed able to cure him. The most famous medicine men of the earth had been called to his bedside. They had invoked their gods and the spirits of their ancestors, they had buried themselves into the earth for three moons without eating or drinking, had died to visit the dead, and had resuscitated themselves. To no avail. Then they tried harder. They swallowed sacred bones, threw themselves into bee hives for days, dived into the river where they lived for two days eating only raw fish, and invoked the wrath of the most devastating tornado. The tornado blew over the village for days and days. Nothing worked.

Village medicine having failed, the white man's doctor was summoned. He studied Zame ya Mebegue. He concluded that Zame ya Mebegue could be cured by his medicine. However, in order for this to happen, the patient had to be taken to the big town, which was the place where the white man had all his sacred magic. The villagers said that such a thing was impossible. They told the doctor that the spirits had gathered one night to choose, among them, the person who would be most able to carry out the sacred duties of pillar and protector of the village. After several hours of debate, the spirits all agreed to appoint Zame ya Mebegue. Zame ya Mebegue had thus become the possessor of extraordinary powers. All his great deeds were the result of the blessings bestowed upon him by the spirits. By agreeing to be powerful, Zame ya Mebegue had given away his own freedom. He was now to live only for his people and for this village. What is more, the spirits said that he could never leave the village, not even for one day. Such a departure, they said, would cause the village to disappear. So, if the white man wanted to cure Zame ya Mebegue, he had to bring his medicine to Zame ya Mebegue.

'Stubborn people!' thought the white doctor. Disappointed, he left them with their sick man and never returned.

Then one day, Zame ya Mebegue himself called the name of Ntole Zame, his elder son.

'Ah Ntole Zame,' he shouted out.

'*Owé! Ah tare!* Pepa!' Ntole Zame responded.

Zame ya Mebegue asked Ntole Zame to summon the village. Last night, he had had a vision. The spirits had come to his headboard to tell him the name of the cure to his disease.

The tom-toms resounded and people travelled from hut to hut to confirm the news and to make sure that everybody would be present. When Zame ya Mebegue summoned the village, nobody was to be absent.

Soon the village was swarming with people, old, young, women, men. Even the village animals stopped running around. Dogs, cats, pigs, chickens and sheep all sat down to listen to the news. Zame ya Mebegue was carried to the *aba* on a *tipoi*.

'My ancestors,' he announced in a moaning and sickly voice, 'visited me last night in my sleep, and told me that only the skin from a wild boar killed by one of my sons could cure me. So, I summoned all of you today to tell you that I am going to send Ntole Zame, my elder son, to the forest to kill a wild boar for me. When I eat the skin of the boar, I will be cured.'

The crowd breathed in relief. 'A wild boar is not that difficult to find,' a few voices said. The forest was full of boars. What was more, Ntole Zame had always been known as a great hunter, just like his father was when he still had his legs under him. 'Well, we are happy. We can finally go home in comfort. Zame ya Mebegue is saved.'

Soon after the meeting, Ntole Zame entered his hut, smeared his body with the magical potion that his mother had concocted for him for such special occasions, put on his hunting garments, and grabbed his *assegai* and gun with the vigour of a soldier ready for battle. He knew what to do. As soon as he was ready, he entered the bush.

Ntole Zame travelled two days and two nights without taking the time to sleep. When he was in his hunting mood, sleep was not a need. All his mind was with the boars. He knew the part of the forest where the wild boars liked to roam. He also knew that, for the cure of his father, he could not come back to the village with just any type of boar. He needed the fattest, most succulent boar. On the third day, Ntole Zame arrived at the banks of the river whose waters the boars liked to drink. This river was known as Ovengwaku, that is 'the place where the Oveng tree falls'. There, he crouched and waited.

Ntole Zame's wait was not too long. When the sun reached the top of the sky, the forest seemed to tremble, as if shaken by an earthquake. Dust soon started to cover all the land around the river, blown by a wind that brought to Ntole Zame the nose-titillating scent of the wild animals. Ntole Zame did not budge a finger. He waited in silence. When the dust finally settled, Ntole Zame could not believe his eyes. Thousands and thousands of boars stood there, drinking thirstily away, seemingly unaware of his presence. Ntole Zame crouched lower, but started to move forward, holding his *assegai* high above his head. He was now able to see the boar he was looking for. He tightened his grip around the *assegai*, ready to throw it. All of a sudden, a voice boomed from amidst the herd. The voice sounded like that of a human, but at the same time like that of a beast. '*Mot!!* A human!!' the voice shouted. The boars scattered in panic. Ntole Zame ran after them, shooting his gun desperately, but without success. The boars crossed forest after forest, clearing after clearing, mountain after mountain, river after river. The chase lasted three whole moons.

Finally, the boars burst into a village. Then, as if in a dream, the boars took off their skins as humans would their clothes. They were now normal humans just like anyone else, except for their skins, which were white like clay. They sat in their *aba* as if nothing had happened. There, they waited.

Ntole Zame followed the tracks left behind by the fleeing herd. He arrived at a river in which he saw fish swimming. He suddenly felt hungry and remembered that he had not eaten for three moons, so taken was he in his pursuit of the animals. He caught the fish, and cooked it on a fire he had lit with his fire rocks. Looking into the river again, he saw that someone had put some *mekoma* in the water to ferment. The now softened cassava pieces would go very well with the fish he had just finished cooking. He took the *mekoma* from the water and ate them with his fish.

After the meal, Ntole Zame resumed his hunt. As soon as he crossed the river he found himself in a village, and found people sitting in the *aba*. This village looked as normal as any other village, except that its people were all white like clay. Ntole Zame knew he had arrived at the village of Bekon, the village of the ghost people. His people often talked of this village, but nobody Ntole Zame knew had ever come back from this village. He would be the first to do so. What an honour!

Zame ya Mebegue's son walked to the *aba* and asked the ghosts if they had seen the herd of boars that he was hunting. They said no. 'How is that possible?' he asked them. 'The tracks I have been following led me straight into your village. Are you going to tell me that you did not see such a huge herd of boars?' The ghosts said they had seen nothing. 'Besides, is that the way you human beings behave?' they asked. 'How can you come into our village and start asking questions without even greeting our elders? Please sit down, you seem very tired. Why don't you sleep here tonight? You could continue your chase tomorrow.'

Ntole Zame agreed and apologized. He told them his story and explained that his father's illness was the reason for his stress. He really needed to find the cure for his father, and it had to be a boar. Only a boar could bring his father from the brink of death. The ghosts told him not to worry. This part of the forest was full of boars. 'You will certainly be able to see some tomorrow morning,' they told him. 'But beware,' they warned, '*Ntol osu, ntol n'vouss*. Elder ahead, elder behind.' 'Why,' wondered Ntole Zame, 'did they say that? I know I am the elder of my mother's belly. But what does it mean, this "elder ahead, elder behind" thing that these people have told me? Is it a riddle? Well, that must just be old people's talk.'

'Ah Ntole Zame!' called the ghosts again.

'*Owé!*' responded Zame ya Mebegue's son.

'You know, in our village here, we have customs for welcoming strangers. Here are twenty of our daughters. Choose one that you would like to spend the night with, one who will be your wife during your stay here with us and who will cook for you.'

Ntole Zame looked at the twenty women who had been lined up before his eyes. They were all as beautiful as river water under sunshine. Their breasts, full and robust, stood on their chests like pointed arrows that seemed to prick Ntole Zame's heart with millions of spears. The curves of their bodies were full with the healthy and sensuous flesh that no man who believes in his manhood can resist. Their smiles offered to him the contours of their voluptuous lips, lips whose flesh seemed ready to be tasted, bitten and then tasted again. The exquisite sight of their teeth as white as clay seemed to taunt him, shining from within mouths that, to Ntole Zame, were no longer normal mouths, but ravines of love. And those eyes! Those eyes seemed to all be begging him: 'Take me! Take me!'

'Why choose one?' he said. 'I will have them all.'

'If such is your choice,' the ghosts said, 'so be it. We cannot refuse anything to our guests, can we?'

'No!' the ghost village echoed in answer.

Ntole Zame spent an incredible night of love with the ghost girls. They cooked for him, nourished him well, and unrestrainedly offered themselves to him well into the middle of the night. Ntole Zame fell into the kind of sleep that even the sound of the fiercest thunder would not manage to scare away. Early in the morning, he was suddenly awakened from his sleep by angry voices from outside his guest hut.

'Look at this useless man,' the voices shouted. 'This man is really without a head. How can someone arrive at a village whose people he does not know, and behave like this? First he arrived at our river, and without asking anyone, ate all of our fish and all of our *mekoma*. Could he not ask for our permission first? Then he comes to our village, and instead of worrying about his dying father, he settles in our place and sleeps with all of our daughters without feeling ashamed. Shame on him! Shame on him! Let him come out so that we can teach him a lesson. What a stupid man this is! What a stupid man this is! Let him come out!'

Ntole Zame could not believe what he was hearing. He looked around. The girls he had spent the night with were nowhere to be seen. In panic, Ntole Zame dressed himself up, took his gun and *assegai*, and ran out to face the angry voices.

What Ntole Zame saw outside was unspeakable. He no longer had a village of ghosts before him, but a village of boars. Thousands and thousands of boars stood in front of his hut. On their faces he could see the signs of murderous anger. Some ghosts, a little farther away, were still coming out of their huts, holding their boar skins in their hands or putting them on as they walked towards the guest hut. A cold shiver shook Ntole Zame. His blood froze in his body.

'Zame ya Mebegue!' He shouted the name of his father in astonishment. 'So, it was you! You were not real boars!'

The boars continued to gather, thousands and thousands of them. The hunter in Ntole Zame soon woke up. He aimed his gun at the closest boars and delivered a thunderous shot. But, suddenly, pfffvvviiiiieeeewwwwwww!! Everything disappeared. No more ghost village, no more boars. Ntole Zame found himself miraculously standing behind his father's hut, in his own village.

'Mmmh! Mmmmh! Mmmmh!' moaned the voice of his sick father. 'Where is Ntole Zame? Mmmmh! Mmmmh! Has Ntole Zame come back yet? Has he come back with the boar skin that is going to cure me? I am suffering so much. Mmmmh! Mmmmh!'

The village gathered to welcome Ntole Zame, only to discover that Ntole Zame's hunt had been a total failure. Ntole did not tell them about the *Bekon* village because he could not remember it. It was as if someone had erased this portion of the story from his memory. His story was simply that he had chased the boars, but had been unable to kill one after three moons spent in the forest. '*Ntol osu, ntol n'vouss*,' some voices said. The crowd dispersed.

The morning after Ntole Zame's return, Zame ya Mebegue summoned the village again, saying that he was now sending Ebara Zame, his second son, into the forest to get a boar skin for him. Ebara Zame promised to do better than his elder brother. So he smeared his body with their mother's concoction, and departed. Just like his elder brother, Ebara Zame tracked the boars down to their village, felt hungry at the village river, ate the fish and *mekoma* that he found, agreed to spend the night at the ghost village and slept with the twenty girls that the ghosts offered him. In the morning, the same angry voices woke him up and when he shot at the ghost-boars, he suddenly found himself behind the hut of his father in his own village. Just like his elder brother, he had failed. '*Ntol osu, ntol n'vouss,*' said some voices in the village upon his return. Again.

Emor Laa Zame, the third son of Zame ya Mebegue, Emor Ñin Zame, the fourth son, and Emor Tan Zame, the fifth son, all went boar hunting and came back empty-handed. They all failed. '*Ntol osu, ntol n'vouss,*' said some voices in the village, again and again.

Zame ya Mebegue is really not lucky, some villagers argued. All his valiant sons have failed to bring him a cure. What is he going to do now? How can a great man like him, a man of such great accomplishments, finish like this? Have the spirits cursed him, or does it just mean that his ancestors have now decided that he should join them? 'Nobody knows, nobody knows,' went the voices.

One morning, at the door of Zame ya Mebegue knocked Osuga Zame, the very last of the great man's sons. No one in the village, not even his father, had thought of him. Osuga Zame was still very young, but at the same time, he appeared not to have his head totally. At times he looked like an idiot, at others he looked like a normal human being. But unlike most boys his age he had never shown any early signs of manhood.

The traps he laid in the forest never caught even a rat. Whereas most children of his age had already successfully hunted ground squirrels, antelopes and monkeys, he, Osuga Zame, had never been able to kill anything. His father and most of the villagers had already, perhaps, dismissed him from the list of sons who were likely to carry on the great name of their father. Had Ntole Zame, Ebara Zame, Emor Laa Zame, Emor Ñin Zame and Emor Tan Zame not been successful in all things prior to their failure with the boars? So, how could Osuga Zame, who had never killed a rat, come back with a boar skin where his brothers had failed?

'Ah *Tare* Zame ya Mebegue,' spoke Osuga Zame as he entered his father's hut. 'I want to go to the forest and bring you the boar skin that you need. Would you give me your blessing?'

Zame ya Mebegue looked at Osuga Zame, and became very thoughtful. 'Ah! My son, my lovely son,' he said to himself. 'I love you very much, perhaps much more than I love any of my other sons. But I also know that you could not possibly accomplish such a risky task. But what can I do? If you have decided that you would like to do it, then I will let you go to the forest. But I have no hope.'

'*Owé!*' Zame ya Mebegue responded. 'My son, if such is your desire, then I will let you go, with all my blessings.'

The village was once again summoned and people were told about Osuga Zame's desire to go boar hunting for his father. How could he succeed where the most valiant sons of his father had failed? village people wondered. 'But if such is his desire, then let him go, and we shall see. But we already know it is useless. He will fail just like his elder brothers.' Other voices, however, were heard saying something else. '*Ntol osu, ntol n'vouss*,' they said. These voices belonged to the elders of the village. 'Elder ahead, elder behind,' they kept repeating.

Osuga Zame smeared his body with the magical concoction of his mother. He dressed himself up in his hunting clothes, took his *assegai* and gun, and entered the forest. After two days and two nights of travel, he arrived at Ovengwaku, the river that was the drinking place of the boars. He crouched and readied himself for the strike. As usual, the wild animals came in a noisy cloud of dust. The sight was impressive. There they were, thousands and thousands and thousands of them, drinking avidly from the river. Osuga Zame lifted his *assegai*, but a voice suddenly boomed from amongst the boars and shouted '*Mot!!*'

The chase began, the boars streaming ahead, Osuga Zame following behind. As usual, the boars took the hunter deep into the forest, crossed river after river, climbed mountain after mountain, and finally crossed the last river. They thus arrived at the ghost village, where they all quickly took off their boar skins and waited in the *aba*. Osuga Zame arrived at the river and saw the fish swimming in the water. He also saw the *mekoma*. He suddenly felt very hungry and wished he could eat this very appetizing fish and these fleshy *mekoma*. 'But,' he thought, 'I do not know to whom these things belong. If there are some *mekoma* in the water, that means that someone lives around here who plants cassava. This fish certainly belongs to that person too, since this river seems to be used by people. Perhaps I should wait until I meet these people and ask them.' Thus, Osuga Zame resolved to continue to track the boars. He crossed the river and, as soon as he set foot on the opposite bank, he suddenly found himself in a village which seemed to have come from nowhere.

The people in the village all looked white like clay, so Osuga Zame supposed that he had arrived in the mysterious village of the *Bekon*. He found a few people sitting in the *aba*. He greeted them and they welcomed him, asking him to join them in the *aba*.

'Our customs,' one of the *Bekon* said, 'require that when foreigners come to or pass through our village we should always offer them good hospitality. Since you are telling us that you are in pursuit of a herd of wild boars, we can only tell you that you need not hurry, for the whole forest around here is full of boars. Be our guest for tonight. Tomorrow, you will continue your hunt.'

'I thank you very much, people of Bekon. I do feel tired, but my father is sick, so I must continue my hunt and rest only after killing the boar needed for my father's cure.'

'Do not worry, young man. We are telling you. This place is full of boars, and we are sure that tomorrow you will see so many of them that you will be able to kill as many as you want. But you see, night is falling and it is better for you not to share the night with the spirits. Sleep here tonight, and tomorrow, continue your hunt.'

'You may be right, my friends. Tomorrow is not far away. I am going to accept your offer since I do feel hungry and tired.'

'Good. Very good, my son,' one of the elder ghosts said. 'But you must know this. Our customs require that we also offer our daughters as wives to the foreigners who spend the night with us. Here are twenty women for you to choose from. They are all very beautiful. You can choose one, or take them all. It is your choice to make. They will take care of you for the night and cook you food. But remember, son, *Ntol osu, ntol n'vouss.*'

Osuga Zame looked at the twenty women. They were like stars shining in a dark night. They were like a gust of fresh air in the smoke of a burning field. They were like drinking cold and fresh water after a hot day of hard work in the bush. Those breasts, eyes, curves, buttocks and lips were like a call to immediate possession.

'I thank you very much, *Bekon* people, for your hospitality. I have only one question to ask you. Are these the only women you have in this place?'

'What do you mean?' the ghosts asked in astonishment. 'Are these women not beautiful enough for you?'

'Oh yes, they are. They are more beautiful than any women I have ever seen. No human woman compares to these. But I am asking if these are the only women you have in this village.'

'Well, no,' the *Bekon* answered. 'All the other women are married. There is only one woman who is left, and we are certain that you will not like this one.'

An elder ghost sent a ghost child to call Oñibot. Her name meant 'Saviour of People'. Oñibot was the ugliest and most repulsive woman Osuga Zame had ever seen. She had been suffering from epilepsy since she was an infant. Furthermore, she was almost blind. She had also suffered from leprosy and, as a result, had lost one arm and one leg. Her remaining arm and leg were not in good shape either since most of her fingers had almost been gnawed away by her terrible affliction. Oñibot spoke only to bark like a dog because she was almost deaf and mute. To make things worse, her body was covered with all sorts of infected and purulent wounds. The smell that came from her body was sickening.

'That is the woman that I want,' said Osuga Zame, pointing his finger at Oñibot.

'Wooooooooh!!' cried the ghosts in amazement. 'What kind of man are you? How can you choose such a pestilence over these voluptuous beauties? However, what can we do? If such is your desire, so be it.'

Osuga Zame spent the night with the pestilent ghost woman. First, he undertook to wash her and clean her up. He then applied some medicine to her wounds and smeared her with sacred oils that would help to heal them. He brushed her hair, cut her few remaining nails and gave her nice clothes. She was now looking much better, and the smell had gone away. Osuga Zame slept on a mat on the floor and gave his bamboo bed to the girl.

In the middle of the night, Osuga Zame was awakened by the voice of the companion he had been given for the night. Oñibot now spoke normally. She did not speak in barks any more.

'Thank you,' said the ghost girl to Osuga Zame. 'Thank you for choosing me over all the others, despite my horrible deformities. Thank you also for washing me and curing my wounds with your medicines. You have done me great good, so I must help you too. The people of my village told you I could not speak. That is not true. But because everybody has dismissed me in this village, I have chosen to be a recluse. Beware, man-who-chose-me, beware, Osuga Zame. This village is not what you think. If you want to save your father, I advise you not to close your eyes in this village at night. Early in the morning, you must be outside in the *aba* before everybody else. Since it will still be dark, no one will see you sitting in the *aba*. The boars you were chasing were not real boars. They were my people. They often disguise themselves as boars with the purpose of luring humans into our village and killing them. No human has ever come back alive from this village. Your brothers were let go simply because they were the sons of Zame ya Mebegue, the only human to whom the spirits had given the power to protect his people against all evils, including the evil of the ghost people. But they made sure none of your brothers would remember their adventures in this village. Tomorrow my people will try to do the same with you. In the morning, they will put on their boar skins and gather in front of your hut, and they will say: "What is this useless man? He arrives at our river, sees fish and some *mekoma*, and he does not even dare to eat them. He comes to our village, we give him twenty beautiful women to spend the night with, but he refuses. He prefers to take a pestilent woman with a missing arm and a missing leg. Where have you seen a man like that before?" After hearing that, you will have to act fast. Shout out the name of your father from the *aba*. My people will all be surprised and will turn towards you. That's when you will have to shoot. Do not hesitate, Osuga Zame. Shoot immediately, and you will succeed.'

Osuga Zame did exactly as the woman told him. He waited in the *aba* very early in the morning. The ghosts came to the front of his hut, dressed in their boar skins. He shouted the name of his father. The boars turned towards him. He fired his gun. A voice came from the crowd of animals: 'Spirits of my people, he has killed us!'

Osuga Zame did not know what happened after that. He suddenly found himself standing behind the hut of his father, with a dead but still warm fat boar at his feet. At his right side stood the most beautiful woman imaginable. This woman was Oñibot, from the ghost village. She had come to the village of the humans with Osuga Zame, to serve him as his wife. She now had two legs, two arms, a very smooth and shiny black skin, and breasts that stood up on her chest like pointed arrows. She was now a normal woman, with curves as sensuous as the most beautiful women Osuga had seen in the ghost village.

As soon as people saw Osuga Zame, they shouted, 'Osuga Zame is back! Osuga Zame has returned! He has brought back with him a wild boar to cure his father. He has also brought back a wife. Wooooh! Wooooh! Osuga Zame has really become a true man. Who would have thought that he would be the one to cure his father? And what a marvellous wife he has, what a sunshine!'

The old people of Zame ya Mebegue's village smiled. '*Ntol osu, ntol n'vouss,*' they thought to themselves. This wisdom has always been true, and they knew it. Elder ahead, elder behind. The one who saves a village is not always the oldest, the strongest, or the richest. The one who saves a village can be the youngest, the weakest, the sickliest or the poorest. No one should ever be dismissed as a fool or an idiot. It is sometimes through the neglected, the excluded and the meekest amongst us that salvation and blessings come to a people. '*Ntol osu, ntol n'vouss*,' the old people kept repeating. The child who saves the family is not necessarily the oldest. When the oldest child fails and thus forfeits his rights of seniority, it is the responsibility of the youngest to take over the role of the elder.

'*Ntol osu, ntol n'vouss*, elder ahead, elder behind,' the old people kept repeating.

'Ah Elang Sima,' she enquired.

'Mema!' I responded.

'Are you listening?'

'*Owé!* Ah Mema. I am listening.'

'Did you hear that story?'

'Yes, Mema. I did.'

Today is a sad day for my mother. I am now six *mimbuh* old, and I am leaving.

'I want you to be my Osuga Zame.'

'*Owé!* Ah Mema. I will be your Osuga Zame.'

'Will you remember, my son? Will you remember?'

'*Owé*, ah Mema, I will remember. '*Ntol osu, ntol n'vouss.*'

I could see tears coming from my mother's eyes and rolling down her cheeks. I did not want to look.

The forest around us was echoing our feeble voices. It was a thick, silent forest. A silence so heavy, so deep it carried to us the hissing whispers of leaves as they conversed with the soft morning wind. From time to time, the astonished voices of monkeys could be heard from far away as they leapt from one tree to the other, probably fighting for some fruits that they did not want to share. From time to time also, the wind brought to us the quarrels of a hundred *gendarme* birds screaming their anger at a snake that had ventured too close to their nests. The echoes of our own footsteps on the road seemed to bring to us the salute of the earth.

This road. I had heard so many stories about this road. This road itself carried on its broken, rain-beaten surface the stories of hundreds of sweaty, torture-broken black bodies, toiling away under the burning equatorial sun. I could see them clearing the bush with their machetes and digging out the road with their hoes. Nested in the back of their minds was the atrocious fear of the deadly whip that never seemed to stop whistling, springing from white hands that obeyed white mouths that never seemed to stop shouting out orders. '*Du nerf, paresseux de nègres! Du nerf!!*' These orders were immediately echoed by a hundred black voices responding 'Heee!' as they lifted their machetes, and 'Han!' as they downed them on the thick undergrowth of the impenetrable rain forest. A number of people from my village, I had learned, had been among those who had built this road with their bare hands while the whip that stroked their backs hastened the pace of their work.

This road. It was now taking me from Otongwaku, my native village, the village of my deceased father, a village that had also been that of his father before him.

My mother was sad. I could see it. I could feel it. It was now a little above three *mimbuh* since she left the *mimbiri* camp where her husband had died. Three *mimbuh* during which the people of her husband ostracized her. They had not spoken to her all this time. And they never stopped accusing her of deliberately taking her husband and two daughters to the *mimbiri* camp to kill and eat them with the other *beyem*. My mother had not spoken to them either. And she never stopped accusing them of destroying her family. She knew someone meaning her harm had eaten up her family so that she would be accused of doing it herself. However, she never let these accusations distract her from the family duties that were now hers alone. She now had to raise her two remaining children on her own and manage the *élik* of her dead man.

So, in spite of the criticism she received, she valiantly

remained in the village of her in-laws. Besides, how could she leave? She was married to this village for life. Our ways did not allow a widow to leave. By marrying my father, she had become a permanent daughter of my father's village. No one, except herself, could chase her from Otongwaku. If she did not want to leave, then no one could do anything about it. She could also choose to remarry with a village man or a man from elsewhere. However, any outsider interested in her would have to come and live with her in her husband's village. He would have to stay here with her and would not be allowed to take her away, unless he repaid the whole of my mother's brideprice to my father's people. But then, our customs were not so simple. A widow with children who belonged to a particular village could not easily leave the *élik* of her husband to go and settle elsewhere with such children. So, simply repaying the brideprice would not solve the issue of the children because it was impossible to transfer children who belonged to a particular village to another man. Children carried in them the blood of the village in which they were born. This blood was sacred and could not be sold away just like that. Because of this, a widow was more likely to remarry and stay in the village of her dead husband than move, unless she was ready to abandon both her children and the *élik* of her husband.

My mother did not want to leave anyway. She did not want to give that pleasure to the sisters of her husband, especially Akoure Okang. That big-mouthed, arrogant sorceress had started to hate her the very first day she came to this village as wife of Sima Okang. The two of them had been like cat and dog and the rivalry had grown worse every day.

I briefly came out of my reveries. The road seemed interminable. It seemed to lengthen its course as we walked over it, pushing back our destination as if refusing to let me go away from my mother.

I looked up and studied my mother's face. The same sad look was in her eyes. This sorrowed look had not left her since the *mimbiri* camp. Something seemed to have died inside her the day when her husband and daughters left us. She had had eyes blurred with tears ever since. Eyes blurred with the bitter tears of daily suffering. Suffering. *Owé!* She knew that word. She had suffered. She had suffered from the harsh reality of a deceased husband who in his death decided to take with him two of their four children, leaving her alone to raise the two remaining boys. And now, one of the boys was leaving.

'Will you remember, my son?' she enquired again. 'Will you remember the story of Osuga Zame?'

'I will remember, Mema,' I replied. Innocently.

We kept walking . . .

They had not talked to her for three *mimbuh*.

Then one day Zula Mebiang, the first child of Akoure Okang, turned up in Otongwaku. He had come to reclaim us, the children of his dead uncle, from my mother. Since my father was the only male from the belly of his mother, a belly that had produced three girls and only one boy, Zula Mebiang, the first son of the family by far, had by tradition become our 'father'. He therefore had the right and the responsibility to take care of my mother and us. Although he was my brother by tradition, Zula was born so early that he was already thirty *mimbuh* when my elder brother was only eight. The difference in age was so huge that he certainly deserved, more than anyone else, the right to be our 'father'. Zula was also an important man. He lived in Beyok, the big city of our country, where he was an employee in the government. By this very fact, he commanded respect, the sort of respect that was similar to that accorded to the white man. His stature and status made people listen to him. A lot of things had been changing in our land. Nowadays, a man who had gone to the white man's school and had a position in the government was more important than our old people. It was now the old people who had to listen to the flawed wisdom of the young, my mother used to complain.

Zula had come from Beyok specifically to summon huge *medzo* in which all the family issues at hand would be resolved, for better or for worse. Of course, Akoure Okang, my aunt, was in total ecstasy. Armed with Zula, her two sisters, and members of the villages to which they had been married, she arrived in Otongwaku with great pomp. Because these *medzo* were going to be huge, there were also people from my mother's family and village, who had come to protect the interests of their daughter. My uncle Otsaga Minlame, as was expected, was present. He was the elder brother of my mother and, although still relatively young, had already earned a reputation for the kind of speaking ability that brought pride and respect to a family. As the people gathered in and around the *aba*, getting ready for the big *medzo*, the shape of the palaver became clear. It would be a three-party *medzo*. Pepa Otsaga Minlame would speak for his village and for my mother, Zula Mebiang would speak for the *élik* of his deceased uncle, and Nkulanveng for the village of my father, Otongwaku, as a whole.

My mother was now humming a sad song as we walked on this road full of history. As if it did not have enough stories to tell already, the road was now recording our story from the rhythm of our steps, the tones of our voices and the feelings of sadness that gripped us. Sometimes, my mother would take my hand and hold it very tight as we walked. Sometimes she would let go of it, as if holding it would cause her to change her mind about my leaving. At other times, she would seem absent-minded, but I knew many thoughts were crossing her mind. The song she was humming sounded familiar. I could not remember where I had heard this song before. It was so sad that it sounded like a song I had heard in church. Or perhaps at a funeral? I was not sure. It could also be a song from one of the hundreds of tales she had told me and my elder brother every night for the past three *mimbuh*. Tales of life, joy and hope as well as tales of death, sorrow and despair.

'*Betare a benane*, fathers and mothers of Otongwaku. *Ma ve mine mbolo!* I salute you!' Zula started that day as the *medzo* began.

'*Mbolo!* We salute you back, nephew of Otongwaku,' responded the crowd.

My mother was sitting silently on one of the bamboo seats that had been set around the *aba* for the *medzo*. She looked subdued. Zula continued.

'I summoned all of you here today so that we can share some time together. It has been such a long time since I last set foot in Otongwaku, the village of my maternal ancestors and uncles. While I am in great joy to see all of you after such a long absence, you also all know how sad I am about the death of my father and the situation that has prevailed in this village since his death. It does indeed sadden me that I should visit you only on such an occasion.'

Zula paused a moment, looking around to make sure that he had started his speech with the right words.

'I know what happened in my absence. I heard some of it while I was away, and more has been told to me since I arrived at Ebang some days ago. What we are going to talk about today is not really very new to you. You know better than I do the events that brought us here today. These events have indeed caused me a lot of grief. Why? Because that woman who is sitting there, that woman for whom we are gathered here today, is also my mother. So, we must make sure that when leaving this *aba* today, we have solved all the issues that have poisoned our family for three years now. From what I have heard, Ntsame Minlame, that woman sitting there, killed . . .'

'*Tebege e vale!*' roared Pepa Otsaga, leaping from his seat like a hungry lion pouncing on its prey. 'I stop you there, young man. I stop you there right now. Do not even let that word come out of your mouth. Killed, you say? Killed whom? Who killed whom? How do you know my sister killed him?'

'I know she did. Why did she have to take my father to the *mimbiri* doctor? Doesn't she know that the white priests have repeatedly warned us against the evil of the *mimbiri* witchcraft? Everyone knows that she took the whole family to the *mimbiri* to have them all eaten up by the *beyem*. That woman is a witch, I tell you. She is an *nnem*.'

'I have told you to shut that mouth of yours, young man,' Pepa Otsaga warned. 'How can you come here and show such a lack of respect for your elders? Is that woman not your mother? Is she not the wife of your own mother? Where have you seen a child speaking to an elder like this? Did the white people's schools you went to teach you disrespect for those who gave birth to you? Did the people in the town you come from teach you that you should come here and talk to us like that? I warn you. I am old, but I swear that I will fight you here today if you continue to show this lack of respect for my little sister.'

The two men stood there for a while, face to face, breathing heavily from their dilated nostrils. Zula finally sat down. So did Pepa Otsaga. The palaver resumed. It was finally agreed that I, the younger of the two remaining children, would go to the big city with Zula. Because the terrible plight that had befallen my mother meant that some *beyem* had decided to exterminate her children, everyone agreed that it might be safer for me to go to the big city with Zula. That way, I would be able to escape the evil that the *beyem* had been planning against my family. Besides, it was well known that the *beyem* feared the white man's electricity. They could therefore not undertake their mystical voyages into town for fear of being burnt to death. My mother would keep Owono Sima, my elder brother, with her. That way, she would not feel too lonely.

Mema.

Mother.

My mother.

For the first time in a long time, my mother did not speak during a palaver. For the first time in a long time, she did not

91

argue with her in-laws. For the first time in a long time, she let others decide her destiny and the destiny of her children. For the first time in a long time, she did not show anyone her machete. She had simply agreed to let me go to the big city.

I was excited. I would be going to school in Beyok, the big town. Everybody dreamt of going to Beyok. But I, I was not just going there, I was going to live there for a few years. Perhaps I would also become someone, someone similar to what Zula had become? A man of the town. A man from the town. A white black man. A black man with power.

Mema.

Mother.

My mother.

I was on my way to Beyok. I was leaving. Oh, Mema. Will you forgive me? Why did you let me go? I am going to Beyok, to become a white black man.

I will remember, mother, I will remember. *Ntol osu, ntol n'vouss.*

The village of Ebang was announcing itself to us. We had walked a long distance, my mother and I. Our feet were sore. We had to take several rests to soothe our feet and drink some water. We were almost there. We could now hear the voices of barking dogs. Soon the village of Ebang itself appeared to us. This was Zula's native village. The village to which his mother Akoure was married. This is where we were going to spend the night before my departure the next day.

The night proved the longest that my mother and I ever spent. We shared the same bed, that night. My mother spent the night awake, crying silently. I could not sleep either. I was too excited to cry. I was excited by the idea of going to Beyok, and this excitement took away the pain I should have felt for leaving my mother. I did not cry. I did not feel any pain. I was too excited. Beyok was already calling me. I was responding.

Early in the morning, a crowd of villagers formed to say goodbye to us. Some gathered in front of Zula's house. Others preferred to walk to the Ntem river crossing for the final farewell. The Ntem was a big river that had no bridge. People and cars crossed it only thanks to a huge old ferry that took them from one bank to the other. Although Zula had a car, he could not drive everybody to the river. So, very early in the morning, many of the villagers trekked to the Ntem river to witness the departure. Zula's departures were always treated as big events. I walked to the river with my mother.

As soon as he arrived at the crossing, Zula drove his car onto the ferry. There, all sorts of foods were loaded and secured on the roof of the car. Soon, everything was ready for the river crossing. Only the passengers were called on board. Zula, his wife, his two sons and I embarked. The engine of the ferry started and the crossing began.

It was there on the moving ferry that, for the first time, I felt the pain. It was there that, for the first time, the crying of my mother reverberated into me, communicating to my body the unbearable agony that this separation was causing her to suffer.

My mother!

Mother!!

Mema!!!

I could now feel the pain. I could feel her pain as I looked at her receding image standing there at the bank of the Ntem river.

94

This was going to be the last image of her that I would have in me for a long time. A painful image.

The engine of the ferry could not suppress the crying voice of my mother. I continued to hear her voice even as we reached the opposite bank of this cruel river. A merciless river that was now separating mother from son. I could still hear my mother crying. I could still see her, even as we now disembarked from the ferry and assembled on the opposite bank to wave a final goodbye before being driven away. My mother's crying voice became louder. We could all hear it. It reached us, loud and painful. The Ntem river was ordering its waters to carry her voice to us, deliberately seeking to augment the pain that I now shared with my mother.

'Mema!' I shouted aloud. Tears were now flowing freely on my cheeks. The river echoed to my mother the sound of my last words to her.

'Mema!'

My mother heard my last call. This proved too much for her. She crumbled to the ground, vanquished by the pain of separation. She cried fiercely. She cried to let everybody know she was losing a child, a child she might never see again. She cried to let everybody know how much she had suffered in life. She cried for her dead husband. She cried for her dead daughters. She cried for death. She cried for life. She cried. I cried. We cried.

We walked to the car.

We drove away.

From the rear seat of the car I looked back, only to see the image of my mother recede even further away from me. It became smaller and smaller. Soon, a bend in the road erased from my eyes the image of her body lying on the muddy bank of the Ntem river, overcome by the pain of, once more, losing a child to destiny.

We reached Beyok after three days of driving. The trip itself was very exciting. This was my very first time in a car. I liked it. This new excitement had already made me forget about my mother. Already.

We reached Beyok at night.

Beyok! The big city. A city full of lights. I had never seen this much light in my whole life. In the village, we used kerosene lamps. These lamps were already a great luxury for us. But this! It was almost like daytime. And all these people! They were everywhere, sleeplessly going about their business.

This was the town in which I would live the next five *mimbuh* of my life. While I lived in Beyok, no one ever brought me news from my mother.

Beyok had conquered my innocent mind. I attended school. I happened to be very good at it.

I liked the white man's school. The white man's school made me forget about Mema. The white man's world was so dazzling, so fascinating that it could make you forget anything! The white man's world was like that. It made you think about things, not people. It made you forget about people. It made you want things. It made you want many things. And when you started to want many things, you had no time left for thinking about people, because you spent so much time trying to get those things that you wanted. So you forgot about everyone. And you no longer cared about anyone else, and no one else cared about you. You were left alone to fend for yourself because everybody else was so busy fending for themselves too. Because of this, many people living in Beyok had forgotten about their villages and their people. The big city made them like that. They simply took to forgetting, because of the big city. And now the big city was causing me to forget too.

Mema!

I had looked forward to coming to Beyok. I had looked forward to those great things that I had heard about Beyok, and how life was great for those who lived in the big city. So, I was ready to conquer the white man's world.

But life in Beyok, at Zula Mebiang's house, was not as easy as I expected it to be.

Zula Mebiang was the son of my aunt Akoure. By tradition, he was my elder brother. But because of the big difference in age that separated his birth from mine, and the fact that his own two boys were of my age group, I was now calling him Pepa Zula.

Zula's wife was a *bilop*, a woman who came from a people who spoke a language different from ours. The rest of the family could communicate with her only in the language that the Fulassi had brought from their land and taught us. Zula's two sons were from a previous marriage which had not worked out. One was exactly my age, and the other was the age of my elder brother. The oldest of Zula's sons had a shrunken, bony and shrivelled arm. The story went that his arm had been eaten by the *beyem*.

My life in Beyok in many ways turned out to be quite the opposite of my dreams. Zula and his wife Alphonsine more or less left it to us to survive on our own. They would both leave for work in the morning and come back only very late in the evening. They would leave us with no food to eat while they were away. On school days we went to classes in the morning and in the afternoon. At noontime all school children had to go home for two hours before returning for lessons in the afternoon. When we came home at noon, we had nothing to eat. When school ended in the late afternoon, we came home to an empty and foodless house. We had to wait for Zula and his wife to come home in the evening before we could have our first meal of the day.

But Zula, I discovered, was also a drunkard. When he came home at night, it was not food that we would get, but the whip. Zula would always come home very late. He would be drunk like a bird with a broken wing. He would often wake us up from sleep and summon us to the living room. Then he would start asking us questions whose heads and toes we did not know. 'Where were you today? Where did you go? How come you are not awake? Who did not go to school? You, Elang?' 'No.' 'So who then? You, Ekang Zula? You did not go to school today, did you?' 'Yes, father, I went to school today.' 'Liar!! Come here! Let me show you who knows the truth!' Then he would call his wife. 'Alphonsine!! Lazy woman! Bring me my black serpent.' The woman would tremblingly come out of their bedroom. She would hand over to him the black belt he used to beat us with. He would start to whip Ekang Zula, his youngest son, to the bone. Then he would turn towards Abogo Zula and me, and administer our dose for the day. Satisfied by the fuss he had created, he would send us to bed. He would order us to stop crying. He would threaten that if we did not stop immediately, he would start whipping us again. We would go quiet. We would be very sore where the belt had designed tracks all over our bodies. '*Vauriens!*' Zula would bark in our direction. Then he would go to sleep, and snore off his drunkenness. In the morning, he would not even remember what he had done.

Since he drank every day, Zula would always find something to reproach us with when he came home at night. And when he did not have anything to hold against us, he would always invent something. 'Abogo Zula!' he would call. 'Pepa!' his oldest son would answer. 'Did you and your brothers take a shower before going to bed?' he would ask. 'Yes,' we would reply. 'Did you use soap to clean yourselves well?' he would continue. 'No,' we would say. 'Why?' he would enquire. 'Because we have no soap,' Abogo Zula would respond. 'What? No soap? Liars!'

And so Zula would get angry, grab his belt and whip us mercilessly for taking a shower without soap. Sometimes, it would be his wife's turn to suffer the wrath of her drunken husband. 'Where were you today? I phoned you at your work and no one knew where you were. And how come no food is cooked? What have you done with your day? Come here!' He would push her in the bedroom, lock the door behind him and start whipping. '*Salope!*' he would insult her, after whipping the poor woman to death. At times she would gather her courage with both of her hands and leave him. But then, after a few weeks, she would always come back. Zula would not even bother to go and beg her back since she always came back on her own when she realized that he would not come. And so she suffered in silence. And so did we.

Because Zula's sons and I had no elder to supervise us during those long school days, we had to invent ways of surviving on our own. When it was still daylight, we would tour our neighbourhood in search of empty beer and soda bottles to sell to bars. Occasionally we would be lucky enough to spot a whole case of empty bottles hidden behind a house. These cases of bottles were worth what, to us, seemed a lot of money. After reconnoitring the terrain, we would eagerly await the night. Once assured that Zula was snoring deeply, we would sneak out of the house and go to steal the bottles we had located during the day. We would always try to make sure no one heard them clink, but unfortunately for us at times we would be heard and the owner would wake up and chase us. We would always manage to escape as we knew our way very well around the slummy neighbourhood we lived in. The money we obtained by selling the bottles would help us to survive for a few days eating bread bought at a local store. When we were lucky enough to find some cooking oil in the kitchen, we would pour this oil in the bread. The result was quite excellent. This was our daily meal. Of course, when it was discovered that the cooking oil was mysteriously disappearing from the kitchen, Zula gave us a beating. We became more careful about stealing the cooking oil after that.

One night, Zula did discover what we were up to. We had taken to going out almost every night to steal bottles spotted during the day, and our outings began to last longer and longer. It happened that on this particular evening, Zula came home a little more sober than he usually did. Because he arrived long after we had gone to bed, he went to sleep without summoning us to his whipping ritual. We expected him to be as drunk as usual, so we got out of the house without knowing that he was still awake. He did not say anything. Since the shithole we used for peeing or relieving our bellies was outside the house, he must have thought we were going out to pee. But a few hours passed and none of us came back. Zula therefore concluded that something was wrong. He got up, checked our bedroom, and finding it empty went outside to see if we were at the family shithole. None of us was in sight. So, Zula quietly came back home, sat down in the darkness outside the house and waited for us.

That night, we stayed out longer than usual. We came home at the crack of dawn to find Zula waiting for us in front of the house, his face tightened with murderous anger. He was holding his black serpent in his hand. He whipped us. For hours, we danced to the whistling tune of the black belt that was lacerating our bodies. Neighbours woke up. They tried to help. Zula waved them away. They watched with tears in their eyes. We cried desperately.

We became more careful with our nightly outings.

I survived Beyok. In some ways I had begun to really like this world of the white man's, above all those things that he taught us at his school. I did very well at school. I was lucky enough to understand very well those things from the world of the white man that our teachers taught us. Zula's sons were less lucky with school. They had hard heads and were unable to absorb things very well. So, I went from one grade to another every year, while they remained in the same grade level for several years. Their father would sometimes become so infuriated with them that he would tie them to poles and whip them in public. The scene would be terrible. I once peed in my pants because I was so afraid that Zula would turn on me and make me share the lot of his children at the poles of crucifixion that he had erected for the sole purpose of distributing punishment.

Surprisingly, Zula did start to develop a liking for me. In his sober moments, he would suddenly start to weep after staring at me. Apparently, I reminded him of his uncle, my father. Whenever visitors came home, he would proudly introduce me to them as the child of his uncle, and tell them about the sacred duty that was his of taking good care of me. A few tears would run along his cheeks as he told his visitors who his uncle was. I would listen very intently.

Zula's shows of affection started to make my life a little harder with his children. They began to feel jealous and to treat me badly. Since we shared the same bed, they would sometimes do weird things to me at night. For instance, they would make me cross my lips and order me to keep them crossed like that. They would threaten to beat me up if I did not obey. At other times, they would pinch me so hard that I would start to cry. They would order me to shut up. Afraid, I would go quiet and accept the torture stoically. Sometimes, Zula would hear me crying. He would ask what was going on. I would say that Ekang Zula and Abogo Zula were bothering me. He would order them to stop or face his belt. They would promise me worse treatment for the next night.

I survived the five *mimbuh* I spent in Beyok. The five years had been filled with good and bad memories. The best memories I got from school, and the good feelings I derived from being number one in my classes. I liked to learn all the things that the teachers had to teach us. I liked the smell of the books we had to read. I liked the different colours of the chalk we used on the blackboard. I liked to be sent to the board to write letters, words and sentences. I liked recreation time when all the children were left to go wild in the schoolyard. It was fun to be running around. It was fun to play with other kids and to share stories, to share our dreams for the future, our dreams for life.

I did not like going home. I did not like going home to the hunger, to the loneliness, to the whip, to Zula. I did not like it. I liked going to school in the morning. I did not like going home in the afternoon.

Beyok.

Beyok was all that. It was bad and it was good. First it was good. Then it became bad. Beyok was all that, bad and good at the same time.

Then one day I was told that we were going back to the village to visit the old people. I would be able to see my mother again. I was happy.

Mema.

Mother.

My mother.

I remember . . .

I do . . .
I try to . . .
Mother!
I had almost forgotten her. Beyok had almost made me forget about her. I was going to see my mother again. I was excited.
Mother!
Mema!

At first, I did not recognize my mother.

I suppose five *mimbuh* is quite a long time for a child who went away at the age of six and who came back only when he was ten or eleven *mimbuh* old. Five *mimbuh* is long enough for a child to forget faces. Long enough for memories to vanish. My mother had been told of my arrival only two weeks after our return. Zula did not take me to her. Eventually, someone was sent to the village where my mother now resided to tell her the news. My mother left immediately for Eboman, the town where Zula's mother, my aunt Akoure, now resided. Akoure's husband, the father of Zula, had died in the village of Ebang while we were away. My aunt thus decided to move to Eboman, where she now had a house. This trip, I later learned, had to do with the death of Zula's father.

At first, I almost did not recognize my mother. I had been away too long, obviously. My mother had arrived while I was outside playing with some newly discovered village friends. Our new village friends saw Zula's sons and me as gods. We had just arrived from Beyok, the big city, with what appeared to them as nice clothes and good looks. Anyone who came from Beyok was always seen as a god. So village children endeavoured to become our friends. In our own way, we were also fascinated by the village children. They knew so many fun things. Village life was so much more fun for the city children that we were than it was in Beyok. Here, we could never get bored because we had so many exciting things to do.

I was busy with some friends running after some sheep when a message came for me. I was told my mother had arrived and wanted to see me. I was happy. I wanted to see my mother again after five years away from her. I ran back to the kitchen house where everyone was waiting for me. I walked in feeling very intimidated by all the eyes that were staring at me. I was hoping to be able to recognize my mother's face among the many faces in front of me. I looked at all the female faces, but could not recognize my mother. I stood there, feeling awkward and not knowing exactly what to do. Fortunately for me, my mother was so impatient to hold me in her arms that she jumped up from her seat, lifted me from the floor and held me tightly in her arms.

'Elang!' she shouted in a broken voice.

'Mema!' I responded.

We stood there in the middle of the kitchen house, holding each other. My mother started to cry profusely. She was shaking with the renewed violence of emotions triggered by past memories that the sight of me had stirred up. She had been holding these tears inside her for the past five years.

I could feel the force of the emotions that now gripped my mother. Unable to resist, I also started to cry. As we stood there in the middle of the kitchen house, my mother and I cried. We cried for the separation that had kept us away from each other for the past five years. We cried for my father, who was dead and whose face I could not remember any more. We cried for the sisters that I would never have. We cried for life. For the sufferings. For the trials of destiny. We cried for ourselves. We cried for the past and the present. We cried for the future. We cried.

When we finally recovered from this first outburst of emotions long contained in the intimacy of our hearts, we looked around us and found tears trickling from the eyes of some of the male and female visitors who had come to greet Zula. They must have felt and shared the pain of the two bodies standing in the centre of the room, bodies broken by five years of absence and separation now offering to their onlookers the emotional scene of their long-awaited reunion.

But my mother's troubles were not over.

Things had gone quite well during the few days my mother had been with us since our return from Beyok. We had got to know each other better again. There were lots of things I did not remember. There were also many things I did not know about – things that had happened while I was away. For example, I learned that while I was gone, she had remarried with a man from another village that had ancestral ties with the people of my village. We were of the same Essangwame clan, so he was almost like a brother to my dead father. But according to my mother, the people of my father's village did not take this marriage very well. They did not accept the fact that the *élik* of my father would become the property of someone from another village, even if that person was from a brotherly village. My mother's man did stay in my father's village for a while, but confronted with the daily animosity of my father's people, they felt forced to relocate to Allen, the village of my mother's new husband.

My mother had many more stories to tell me, but could not recount all of them on this short visit. This was, she told me, her initial visit. It was a courtesy visit meant to greet us. For the occasion, she had brought a pig and a few chickens that had been slaughtered in my honour. She cooked these animals and as she was an excellent cook people feasted on them for two days, whether or not they had been invited. After a stay of about a week, my mother left us. She told me she would come back later to get me.

Village life was strange, but very exciting. Ekang Zula, Abogo Zula and I roamed around, making new friends and chasing goats all over the village. We were excited by the new village experience and were eager to explore even more. We also discovered some of the harsh aspects of village life. Water had to be fetched from springs far away in the forest and it was mostly the task of children and women to do this. We thus got our share of hard labour as we travelled the distance to and from the spring several times a day, carrying buckets on our heads.

We did not like this very much, but we did not have a choice. Everybody needed the water. It was needed for drinking, cooking and washing. Only the elders were allowed to use the water for washing: children had to go to the river to wash themselves. The job of fetching the water was especially hard for us because this was the long dry season when water was hard to find. This season also coincided with the long school vacation when children had to stay home for two months. So, we were always available and could not escape from our water-fetching duties. We had to make several trips and fill up several containers daily before water was deemed sufficient for everybody. We usually washed ourselves on the last trip home. Although we did not like this chore at first, we gradually got used to it.

When it rained, we took a break from getting water for the elders to wash with because rain water could be collected instead. We thus only had to fetch cooking and drinking water.

This made our lives a little easier at times, but only at times because the rains were scarce during the big dry season.

But water-fetching was fun too. As we got used to the new routine of village life, we came to enjoy certain aspects of the activity. On our way to the spring, we made friends and met nice village girls. We made plans to go to the bush to hunt squirrels and birds with our small catapults; we often laughed at ourselves when fetching water because, after a rainy day, the hilly and muddy path to the river was very slippery and we often fell to the ground, thus losing our precious cargo of water. Some of us sometimes had to return to the river several times before being eventually able to defeat this untameable path of doom. In the end, it all became a great game for us.

The water-fetching trips and other activities in which we took part became a great learning experience during which village children taught us the fun aspects of life in the village. It was the village children, for example, who taught us how to hunt the ground squirrel. This strange squirrel was not like any others. First of all, it did not live in trees like other squirrels. Although I am sure it could climb trees and get palm nuts from palm trees, this weird squirrel ate mostly on the ground. Furthermore, it lived in underground caves that it would dig out and use as a home and a place to store palm nuts for consumption during the dry season. The ground squirrel was also bigger than the normal, tree-dwelling squirrel and looked more like a giant rat that could reach the size of a well-nourished cat. The ground squirrel was also a very clever animal. It always dug its caves with security in mind. Because it knew it had several enemies – snakes and little humans like us – it would always dig caves with both an entrance and an exit. The entrance was always very visible and could be easily spotted in the bush. But the exit was always hidden and not completely dug out. At times the squirrel would even dig several such exits, just in case things turned out to be more dangerous than expected. So, when a life-threatening emergency presented itself, the clever beast would simply shoot out like a bullet from any of the hidden exits of its cave and thus escape from death. When expertly cooked by our mothers in the village, with an assortment of aromatic leaves and spices, the ground squirrel was one of the most delicious meats, particularly relished by children. Fights among children were not uncommon when it came to deciding which part of the animal was going to be eaten by whom, and who would get to lick clean the bottom of the pot.

To hunt the ground squirrel, the village children had to organize themselves into a small army. A band of at least ten was often necessary to ensure success. There was always a self-appointed general who claimed to know everything about ground-squirrel hunting, giving himself credit for having led to the killing of several hundred of this animal. Of course, we had to take his word for it and follow his orders. The general would order us to gather the necessary weapons. Shovels, machetes and hoes were the primary instruments. They were to be used for digging the trenches. We then had to arm ourselves with thick and heavy sticks to be used as clubs for the final assault on the squirrels. We also needed matches and dry leaves for lighting a fire at the mouth of the cave if need be.

When everything was ready, the troops would depart for the battlefields in the bush. On the paths that led us deeper into the forest, strategy was discussed. We had to choose between doing battle in a cocoa field or in a field of peanuts. The cocoa fields were attractive to some of us because while hunting we could help ourselves to the creamy juice of the cocoa fruits. But cocoa fields had the inconvenience of needing to be cleared. Others among us thought the peanut fields were better, because while battling we would be able to enjoy some of the sugar canes that the owners of the fields had so generously planted, unsuspecting as they were of the invasions that were to be conducted on these very grounds by hungry young warriors in pursuit of squirrels. Indeed, if the owners ever discovered us wreaking havoc in the fields . . .

We usually chose the peanut fields because they lent themselves to easier pursuits, most obstacles having been cleared by the owners. Once in the field, we proceeded, as good warriors should, to secure the territory. We would look for the best possible squirrel hole in the ground. We knew a hole was good when it showed signs of recent activity. Usually, the mouth of a frequently used ground-squirrel hole would look slick, polished and shiny. No spider webs and no leaves would be blocking its entrance. Next, we would look for the enemy's exit holes. These were usually situated quite a few feet away from the main entrance hole. The clever animal usually made his exit holes so small that it took great care and scrutiny to discover them. But we were warriors, were we not? We knew how to reduce the enemy's tactics to nothingness. Its exit holes would be quickly unveiled and three soldiers with heavy wooden clubs positioned at each one, ready to strike at the slightest sign of movement. Two or more soldiers would be posted on guard around the place, just in case the enemy should shoot out from a hidden hole that we had missed. It was now time to think of a strategy for the attack.

We had two choices. We could set a few dry leaves on fire at the entrance of the main hole, or, before doing so, dig along the network of tunnels towards the enemy. Strategically, digging first was always better because we were never sure how the tunnels were laid out. Sometimes they went down very deep, only to climb up abruptly, bifurcating left or right. But there was more. The enemy was expert at building barricades with used nuts. These kept away common predators like snakes and could protect against smoke. So, the best course of action for us

113

was to dig along the tunnels first, smashing down the few barricades that the enemy had erected along the way. As we drew closer, and became convinced that there would be no more barricades between the enemy and us, we would set dry leaves on fire and vent the smoke into the remaining portions of the dark tunnels.

Our enemy was not a simple, unsophisticated enemy. He was one who used very elaborate evasion tactics. One would think that, with all the noise and commotion caused by our digging, he would panic and rush out. Not at all: he would remain quiet and seemingly unmoved. His thinking was clear to us. He was, up to the last minute, hoping that we would assume the cave empty and give up. But we were used to such tactics and we knew how tenaciously the enemy often held his ground.

But we still had to be careful because there were times when, unexpectedly, the enemy would surprise us. Instead of coming out from where we expected him to, the animal would seek escape through the main hole and rush out from right between the legs of the digger. Taken aback, the digger would fall flat on his buttocks, and the beast would escape, leaving us totally confused and panicked. At that point, trying to regroup the troops would be of no avail as the enemy would quickly disappear into the bush. This is why, learning from his past experiences, the general always positioned a warrior behind the digger, just in case.

The soldiers would relieve each other at the digging post, taking turns. The club holders would nervously take a firmer grip on their weapons as the digging came closer to the enemy's secret chamber. Meanwhile, if we chose to light a fire, the smoke would seethe through the catacomb. From then on, we would be ready for anything.

As expected, the enemy would come shooting out from one of the guarded exits. The soldiers would respond with heavy blows and would launch into the pursuit of the fleeing enemy. Sometimes, when we were lucky, it would be a whole family of ground squirrels rushing out. But knocking out the enemy with our clubs was never an easy job. Precision was not necessarily our strength. The enemy would sometimes escape our blows and disappear into the bushes. But most of the time, we were able to deal the fatal blow. Thus, in the afternoon, exhausted but happy after repeating successful assaults against a few more enemy strongholds, we would go back to the village. Our bounty would be proudly hanging from the shoulders of the general, who had claimed for himself the honour of carrying the battle spoils. The evening feast would be great for all, young and old.

My mother came back to Eboman two weeks later. I saw in her demeanour that she had come readied for battle. Once more. But, as was customary, she had sent a message warning of her arrival, and had requested that, on the appointed day, everybody be there so that a *medzo* session could be held. I did not know what the *medzo* was about, but I knew that lots of people had gathered. I also knew that a few days before, I had been coached by *nnah* Akoure, who told me that if my mother asked me to leave with her, I should start to cry and roll on the floor. That way, my mother would not dare to take me away. I agreed to the idea, not knowing exactly why I had to do that. And here we were, in *nnah* Akoure's kitchen house again. There was, of course, Zula himself, but also his mother *nnah* Akoure. Lots of other relatives had gathered in support of Zula and his mother. My mother had come alone.

Alone. Oh, Mother. Oh, Mema. Lonely. So lonely. My mother had come alone, and she was ready for battle. I could see this in her eyes.

'I greet all of you,' began my mother as she sat by my side on a bamboo bed. 'I thank you all for attending this *medzo*, and I thank Zula for the good care he took of my son. I can see that my son came back from Beyok with a good body, and I am grateful for that.'

She paused a little bit, looking around her, as if expecting that what she was going to say next would be disliked by her listeners. I had a strong sense, at that moment, that people knew

116

what she was going to say, and that she was right: they would not like it. After a short silence, she continued:

'Five *mimbuh* ago, I gave Zula my son, so that he could take him away with him to Beyok. My decision to give my son away was a hard one, but I knew that this was the best thing to do if I was to protect him against the evil that had eaten both my husband and my two daughters.'

My mother's voice broke down upon uttering these words. A few tears trickled down her cheeks. She managed to contain herself.

'Now, a few weeks ago, I came to greet Zula and my son. I was hoping that Zula would see that I was missing my son very much, and that he would let me have him. Unfortunately, he did not. Because I did not want to cause any trouble, I left quietly. I wanted my son to have the time to enjoy his return. During the past two weeks, life has been hellish for me. I waited for a sign from Zula telling me to come and get my child. But nothing came. Now, the question I am asking all of you standing here is the following: must I be a stranger to my own child? Must I be to him a simple visitor who has to ask for Zula's benediction in order to see him?'

She paused and looked at me, taking my hand. Then she continued:

'In the past few days, I have asked myself what I have done to the gods to deserve such a lot. I have asked myself why my husband's people have elected to trouble me so much. Must my life in this world be miserable simply because I lost my husband to death? Ah Zula! When I gave you my child five years ago, did I say I was giving him away to you for ever? No. I said to you: "Son, here is your little brother. Take good care of him and bring him back to me as healthy as I gave him to you." Since your return, you have been behaving like someone who did not want to give me my child back. You have been insulting me, the mother of this child, by treating me like a stranger who had no right to that child. So, I have come to tell you that, today, I am taking my child home to Allen with me.'

Zula stood up and cleared his throat. His eyes were red with the anger of someone who was ready to kill.

'Woman,' Zula began, 'I have heard what you have said. But I can already tell you this. Elang will never leave my house to go back with you. Are you forgetting the past? Are you forgetting that you are the same woman who took my uncle to the *mimbiri* doctor to kill him? Not only did you kill him, but you also killed your two daughters. And now, you want to take one of his last two children to sell him away to the *beyem* of your new husband's village? No, mother. As long as I am alive, this child will stay with me. It is my responsibility, as the first son of this family, to protect my uncle's *élik*. And I tell you already, Elang will not go to Allen with you. In fact, I did not bring him to stay. I came back here only to take care of the ceremonies required for my father's death. I will be returning to Beyok soon and Elang will go with me.'

My mother sprang from her bamboo seat like a famished she-lion. She slapped Zula in the face, causing him to step backward and tumble against his seat. He landed squarely on his buttocks, causing panic among the people who were sitting behind him.

'I have had enough!' my mother shouted fiercely. 'I tell you this right now. I have had enough. I will not take the disrespect of this man any more. Ah Zula. Are you forgetting who you are talking to? Are you forgetting that I once cleaned shit from your buttocks? Who gave you the right to talk to me with such disrespect? Did anyone say to you that working in Beyok in the white man's world gave you the right to come here and insult me? Today, I will show all of you that I am Ntsame Minlame.'

Upon this, my mother turned towards me and called: 'Elang!'

'Mema,' I responded, trembling.

'Get up and let's go!' she commanded. I hesitated, not knowing what to do. I was afraid. I looked at her, then looked at my aunt Akoure. Then, I remembered that I had to start crying and roll on the floor. I did. My mother was not deceived. She briskly seized my arm, pulling me from the floor towards her. Zula had finally been helped up. He and his mother advanced, intending to pull me away from my mother.

'*Song!*' shouted my mother, in a chilling voice that froze Zula and his mother on the spot. In her hand had miraculously appeared a machete. The crowd that had gathered inside and outside the kitchen house dispersed in panic.

My mother walked out, pushing me in front of her. 'Let's go,' she repeated. We walked out. We did not look back. My mother still had the machete in her hand. No one came after us. I did not look back. I did not go back to Beyok with Zula.

Mema.

Mother.

My mother.

I came to know my mother well over the years. I came to admire the incredible woman that she was. I now loved her to death and I was ready to defend and protect her against all enemies.

Mema.

Mother.

My mother.

◆

My mother, I now realize, was an intelligent woman. She had the power to keep me with her if she so desired, but she knew that keeping me with her in our poor village would not, in the long run, prove valuable in the new world that the white man was slowly creating for us. She knew that true power, in the world now developing before her eyes, would reside only with those who had been to the white man's schools. Zula Mebiang had been to the white man's school. As a result, he had enormous power not only in his own village, but also in the village of my father. Because of his status as a man from Beyok, Zula was an important figure. Serious village matters were never tried until Zula came from the big city to attend such *medzo*. All would look up to his wisdom, which now overshadowed that of the elders, be they men or women. Only my mother, that rebellious woman, would not let Zula have his way. As I think back to those days, to my departure for Beyok on that ferry, to the receding shadow of my mother crying over the gulf of separation that the Ntem river was becoming, I now realize that my mother was not giving in to any pressure. She knew what she was doing when she painfully gave me away to Zula Mebiang. She knew what she was doing when, at that village *medzo* that decided her final lot, she silently agreed to give me away.

My mother knew that going to Beyok, the big town, would give me schooling. With schooling would come power, and with power total protection for her and my elder brother. She knew I would become the protecting force, the shelter for both herself and my elder brother. My mother knew that the white man's school would make me the Osuga Zame of the family. '*Ntol osu, ntol n'vouss*,' she kept repeating to me over the years.

I will remember, Mother. I will remember.

My return to the village and staying with my mother did not change her resolve. She planted peanuts, sold cassava, and saved the money that allowed me to continue to go to school. I promised my mother I would continue to go to school and drink at the fountain of strange knowledge that the white man had come to build on our land. I promised her that I would learn and become someone in this white man's world. That was the only way out. That was the only way of protecting oneself in the new world that was taking shape before our very eyes. A strange world, where the elders were becoming dependent upon the youth and where the youth were becoming the administrators of wisdoms coming from foreign lands. It was a new world in which our people no longer knew their own wisdoms, because the wisdoms of the white man had prevailed. The wisdoms of the white man had prevailed because they made our people forget their own wisdoms. When you learned the wisdoms of the white man, you forgot your own. The white man knew how to make you forget your own people and your own wisdoms. It was that world that I was entering now. Because I promised. I promised her I would. And I promised I would not forget. I promised I would remember. I could not afford to forget. I had to remember. For her. I did. She won.

Mema.

Mother.

My mother.

I remember, Mother.

Mema, I remember.